Putting
Transform
Century

MW01504318

t

The Internet is like a 20-foot tidal wave coming, and we are in kayaks. Some are more aware of this than others.

Andy Grove, July, 1996.

David D. Thornburg, Ph.D.
DThornburg@aol.com
http://www.tcpd.org

Thornburg, David D.
Putting the Web to Work: Transforming Education for the Next
Century

ISBN 0-942207-12-2 (pbk.)
Copyright © 1996 by David D. Thornburg and Starsong
Publications

Published in the United States of America.

ISBN 0-942207-12-2

Dr. Thornburg can be contacted at:
Thornburg Center
P. O. Box 7168
San Carlos, CA 94070
415-508-0314
DThornburg@aol.com
http://www.tcpd.org

Dedication

It is an honor to dedicate this book to the memory of Dr. Vannevar Bush, a gifted scientist and visionary whose image of the future has now become a reality.

Thank you for giving us dreams we could catch in our Web.

Vannevar Bush, Ph.D.

Contents

Preface

Writing a book about something changing as rapidly as the World Wide Web is a bit like trying to swap an engine out of a race car while it is zooming around the track. I started this book in 1995, hoping to complete it by October of that year. These words are being written in 1996. I did not delay in the futile hope that developments in this area would slow down — in fact, they have accelerated. My delay was caused by the fact that every time I would write a chapter, I'd find that my predictions for the future had already come true.

I finally made peace with the fact that, by definition, some of the content would be out of date by the time the book appeared in print.

My goal is not to present up to the minute information, but to present information of long-term value exploring the incredible phenomenon of the Web and its impact on virtually every aspect of how we learn. The Thornburg Center's Web site (http://www.tcpd.org) is a place where new perspectives are posted for those wanting to stay up to date.

My previous book on the telecommunications revolution, *Education in the Communication Age*, had almost nothing to say about the Web. At the time it was written, the Web was in emergence. In the past year it has jumped into everyday speech and "URL's" (Web addresses) appear on everything from television advertisements to the front pages of newspapers.

To resist the temptation to keep tweaking the content, I formulated the overall plan for this book in Brazil and wrote most of it in our Monterey and San Francisco offices — places where I could escape from the tyranny of the urgent.

Before embarking on our journey together, a few comments are in order: Any Web sites we mention worked the day this book was sent to press. The Web is a dynamic medium, and some of the places we send you may have moved. Also, software we recommend may have undergone revisions since this book was published, so be on the lookout for the most recent versions of any tools we mention.

Finally, you'll see comments in this book about various companies whose technologies we find interesting. The Thornburg Center, as a technology futures research group, looks at many emerging technologies. Our evaluation criteria have nothing to do with whether these companies are good investments. We may or may not hold investments in some of the companies mentioned, so we do not recommend stock purchases or provide financial advice of any kind. If you want to evaluate the investment potential of any company we mention, please contact your broker.

And, one last note: Throughout this book you'll see references in the form of URL's. Ours, for example, is http://www.tcpd.org. When you encounter one of these you can type it into your Web browser and (assuming you have an Internet connection) you'll be taken directly to the referenced site. All of the references in this book are posted on the Thornburg Center site (at http://www.tcpd.org/ webwork.html) where you can simply click on them, instead of having to type them in. This list can be saved on your computer for use anytime you want to explore the places we've identified.

David Thornburg, Rio de Janeiro, San Francisco, Monterey, 1996.

New Tools for a New Age

Two years ago, if you wanted a graphical user interface to computer-based telecommunications services from your home, you needed an account with America Online or one of the other proprietary on-line service providers. If you wanted to access the Internet directly from a standard telephone line, you probably used a text-based interface whose commands resembled MS-DOS on steroids. While the rest of the computing world was moving toward point and click, the Net was still largely text-based — at least for most of us.

What changed? Was it a breakthrough from Apple, or Microsoft?

No — it came from Marc Andreesen, a $6.75 per hour programmer/college student nestled in America's heartland at the University of Illinois' Supercomputer Center. His work was built on earlier foundations, so a bit of history is in order at this point.

Back in 1989, Tim Berners-Lee at the Swiss research lab, CERN, invented the World Wide Web (which we will refer to as the Web). His main goal was to provide a way for scientists to share documents and research with their peers using "hypertext." A hypertext document contains links that can take the user to other places in the same document, or even to other documents.

The original idea for hypertext appeared in an article by Vannevar Bush in the July, 1945 issue of Atlantic Monthly (http://www.theAtlantic.com/atlantic/atlweb/flashbks/computer/bushf.htm). In his article, "As We May Think," Bush described a hypothetical machine called a "memex" that would contain documents filled with rich links to other documents. Users could navigate within and between documents, making links of their own as they researched any topic of interest. As you read the excerpt below, think about how accurately Dr. Bush anticipated the future — and then remember that this article was published one year before the Eniac, one of the first general purpose digital computers, was turned on for the first time!

The human mind ... operates by association. With one item in its grasp, it snaps instantly to the next that is suggested by the association of thoughts, in accordance with some intricate web of trails carried by the cells of the brain. It has other characteristics, of course; trails that are not frequently followed are prone to fade, items are not fully permanent, memory is transitory. Yet the speed of action, the intricacy of trails, the detail of mental pictures, is awe-inspiring beyond all else in nature.

Man cannot hope fully to duplicate this mental process artificially, but he certainly ought to be able to learn from it. In minor ways he may even improve, for his records have relative permanency. The first idea, however, to be drawn from the analogy concerns selection. Selection by association, rather than indexing, may yet be mechanized. One cannot hope thus to equal the speed and flexibility with which the mind follows an associative trail, but it should be possible to beat the mind decisively in regard to the permanence and clarity of the items resurrected from storage.

Consider a future device for individual use, which is a sort of mechanized private file and library. It needs a name, and, to coin one at random, "memex" will do. A memex is a device in which an individual stores all his books, records, and communications, and which is mechanized so that it may be consulted with exceeding speed and flexibility. It is an enlarged intimate supplement to his memory.

...

The owner of the memex, let us say, is interested in the origin and properties of the bow and arrow. Specifically he is studying why the short Turkish bow was apparently superior to the English long bow in the skirmishes of the Crusades. He has dozens of possibly pertinent books and articles in his memex. First he runs through an encyclopedia, finds an interesting but sketchy article, leaves it projected. Next, in a history, he finds another pertinent item, and ties the two together. Thus he goes, building a trail of many items. Occasionally he inserts a comment of his own, either linking it into the main trail or joining it by a side trail to a particular item. When it becomes evident that the elastic properties of available materials had a great deal to do with the bow, he branches off on a side trail which takes him through textbooks on elasticity and tables of physical constants. He inserts a page of longhand analysis of his own. Thus he builds a trail of his interest through the maze of materials available to him.

And his trails do not fade. Several years later, his talk with a friend turns to the queer ways in which a people resist innovations, even of vital interest. He has an example, in the fact that the outraged Europeans still failed to adopt the Turkish bow. In fact he has a trail on it. A touch brings up the code book. Tapping a few keys projects the head of the trail. A lever runs through it at will, stopping at interesting items, going off on side excursions. It is an interesting trail, pertinent to the discussion. So he sets a reproducer in action, photographs the whole trail out, and passes it to his friend for insertion in his own memex, there to be linked into the more general trail.

Wholly new forms of encyclopedias will appear, ready made with a mesh of associative trails running through them, ready to be dropped into the memex and there amplified. The lawyer has at his touch the associated opinions and decisions of his whole experience, and of the experience of friends and authorities. The patent attorney

11

has on call the millions of issued patents, with familiar trails to every point of his client's interest. The physician, puzzled by a patient's reactions, strikes the trail established in studying an earlier similar case, and runs rapidly through analogous case histories, with side references to the classics for the pertinent anatomy and histology. The chemist, struggling with the synthesis of an organic compound, has all the chemical literature before him in his laboratory, with trails following the analogies of compounds, and side trails to their physical and chemical behavior.

The historian, with a vast chronological account of a people, parallels it with a skip trail which stops only on the salient items, and can follow at any time contemporary trails which lead him all over civilization at a particular epoch. There is a new profession of trail blazers, those who find delight in the task of establishing useful trails through the enormous mass of the common record. The inheritance from the master becomes, not only his additions to the world's record, but for his disciples the entire scaffolding by which they were erected.

As these passages show, Vannevar Bush predicted much of the world we now experience through the World Wide Web!

Originally, the Web was text-based, but the basics were there. The key was the creation of a special document description language called "HTML" (Hypertext Markup Language). This text-based language is used to describe pages, specifying headings, citations, new paragraphs, and other page layout information in a form that could be transmitted for interpretation on virtually any computer platform. While the special "tags" indicating various features of the document are a bit arcane, most of them can be mastered in a short time, making it possible for anyone to create Web documents (called "pages") of their own.

In addition to describing the physical structure of a document, HTML provided tags for links within the same document or to other documents anywhere on the Internet they might happen to be. These links form the basis for hypertext.

Marc Andreesen, then a student at the University of Illinois, realized the power of links could be increased by extending them to graphics. Mosaic, the first graphical Web browser, was born in 1993.

As the Web became easier to use, its use exploded. While the Internet itself was doubling in size every year, the Web started doubling every 90 days — a pace it has maintained ever since. This rapid growth is shown in the following chart from Webcrawler (http://www.webcrawler.com).

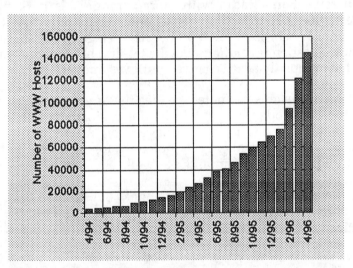

In 1995, Netscape — the company built around Marc Andreesen's current activities — went public, having already captured the number-one spot as the provider of both browser and server software for the World Wide Web.

Meanwhile, proprietary services like e-World, Prodigy, Compuserve, and AOL found that they needed to move quickly to provide Web access to their customers, or risk going bankrupt. For e-World, the move came too late, and the other three services have been doing everything in their power to address consumer demand for Web access.

In the span of two years, the Web catapulted from a little-known service into the mainstream of our consciousness. A survey by A. C. Nielsen (http://www.nielsenmedia.com/whatsnew/execsum2.htm) found that Americans spend more time on the Internet than they do watching rental video tapes. Find/SVP (http://etrg.findsvp.com) found that 35% of all adult Internet users have reduced the time they spend watching television — by as much as 20%.

Is this interest in the Web a fad? Is it, as one pundit said, "Citizen's Band Radio with more typing?" Is it rising in interest like a Fourth of July rocket only to burn out when it hits its peak? Or is the Web the next stage in a series of communication revolutions like the telegraph, telephone, radio, and television that each changed our lives forever?

Sun Microsystems promotes the idea that if your business isn't on the Web today, you might be out of business tomorrow. While this may be a bit of an exaggeration, it isn't far from the mark. And the challenge is not only for business, but for education and our communities as well.

We'll explore many ideas in this book, but first we'll look at what you'll need to access the Web — to become a full-fledged Netizen in Cyberia.

Getting Connected

You'll need the following things to connect to the Web:

1. A personal computer
2. A modem
3. An account with an Internet service provider (ISP)
4. A "Web browser" and other support software

Let's look at each of these items:

Your computer
You'll need a modern personal computer (color graphical display preferred). Just about anything on the market today will work. The three dominant platforms used for Web access are the high-end UNIX machines, the Macintosh platform, and the "Wintel" computers typified by the offerings of Compaq, IBM, Dell, etc. Most Web servers run under the UNIX operating system, and computers by Sun and Silicon Graphics tend to dominate that field. Most Web authoring is done using Macintosh computers, and there are wonderful authoring tools available for that platform.

If you are primarily going to use the Web for research and general exploration, just about any current platform will work. To be safe, just be sure that the computer you use runs the latest version of Netscape Navigator (http://home.netscape.com). This will insure that your computer has enough power to explore the rich realms of information available on the Web, as well as to run special Web-based programs written in a language called Java (http://java.sun.com).

Java was developed by a team from Sun Microsystems to add an incredible array of capabilities to the Web. While Java programs reside on remote sites, they are automatically downloaded to your computer, as needed, where they run on your system. Because Java programs are interpreted by your browser software, they will run on just about any modern computer, independent of its operating system.

To get the best performance from the Web, and to anticipate new tools and features that will be released in the next year, you'll find truth in the adage that you can never be too thin or have too much RAM.

What about the "$500 Network Computer" (NC)?

As this book was being written, a huge debate was taking place in the press regarding an announcement from Oracle's Larry Ellison (http://www.oracle.com) and Sun's Scott McNealy (http://www.sun.com) of a $500 "Network Computer" (or "NC" as it is now known). The initial announcement was not of a product per se, but of the idea that such a product would revolutionize our use of the Internet when it became available.

This technological marvel was going to change life as we knew it: It would become a powerful tool in our informational arsenal and bring the miracles of the Web to the majority of Americans who think a space bar is a snack food served on shuttle flights.

While over 30% of our homes are equipped with computers, only a fraction of those are wired to the Web. The NC would change all that. By providing easy access to the Web, Java applets, and the other info-goodies we early adopters were growing to know and love, McNealy and Ellison hoped to send a shockwave throughout the industry, and specifically to Prince William Gates of Redmond.

As the idea began to spread that the Sun just might set on the Gatesian universe, the pundits pecked out their opinions regarding NC's. The broadsides bellowing chastisements of the concept were numerous. Even otherwise intelligent commentators like Stewart Alsop (http://www.infoworld.

com) had something negative to say about the network appliance.

Bill Gates (http://www.microsoft.com) initially declared the idea idiotic ... until he realized that there was a way for him to make money from it. Now he seems content to sip from his cup of Java while pondering his next move.

The main arguments against the NC fell into a few predictable categories:

- First was the notion that this was a tool for moving headlong into the past — a retrograde shift to the era of the "dumb terminal" and the "glass teletype." By suggesting that the heavy lifting would be done on centralized remote servers, detractors argued that the NC was nothing but a move back to the mainframe era.

What they missed was that the servers were not going to be doing much of the computing. Java programs would be shipped to the user's computer where they would run on the local processor.

The time-shared mainframe specter had died long ago, but some writers felt it was now limping back to life.

They are wrong.

- Other detractors argued that, "If we can make a PC that retails for $500, why haven't we already done it?"

Again, this misses the nature of the NC. Its job is not to run bloatware, but to access the Web. A few custom chips can handle this task quite well, and still provide the functionality found in the latest versions of Netscape (http://www.netscape.com) with a folder full of plug-ins.

Will it run Word 6.0? Of course not, but neither will my PowerPC. The unholy alliance of Gates and Grove has conspired to insure that any computer you purchase will appear ungainly within six months so you can justify getting a new one.

- The argument I find most interesting is that "People won't give up their PC's to use these devices."

The NC isn't designed to replace a PC — it is a beast of a different color altogether, and they both have a place in the world.

There are lots of circumstances for which a specific single-purpose machine can have tremendous utility — enough utility to justify its purchase. For example, I have a fax machine in my office, even though I also have fax software on my computer. I find the fax machine worthwhile because I'm not willing to tie up my $3,000 desktop machine for a function served quite well by a $300 fax.

By the time you read these words, the NC will be a reality. One of these inexpensive machines might be just the ticket for you. If you need a computer for other tasks, or you wish to create your own Web pages, then you'll want to stick with a traditional personal computer. As a tool for doing research on the Web, though, the NC should prove very handy. For some users, it is the only machine they will need.

If you want to keep up on developments in this field, be sure to visit http://www.nc.ihost.com.

Your modem

In addition to your computer, you'll need a modem or some other method for connecting to a communications line. The job of a modem is to translate the digital data stream from your computer into a series of analog tones (somewhat like musical notes) that can be sent over voice-grade telephone lines. The process of converting the digital data to tones is called "modulation," and the reverse process (needed at the other end) is called "demodulation." Since your computer will both send and receive data, you need a device that performs both tasks. "Modulation" and "demodulation" have been shortened to "modem."

If you purchased your computer recently, it might have a built-in modem. If not, then you'll need to buy one. Generally your choice is either to get an external modem that connects through a cable to your computer's serial port, or to get a modem that plugs into a slot inside your computer. Many portable computers accommodate "PC Card" modems that plug into the computer through a slot in the side of the case.

I used to strongly recommend that people get external modems, since modem speed was increasing every year or so, and you could upgrade to a new one without having to open up the case. Today the most popular modem speed is 28.8 kb/sec, and this is probably about as fast as you'll be able to send data reliably over a voice-grade phone line. (Please don't quote me on this when the speed doubles in a year!) If you decide to install a built-in modem operating at this speed, you'll probably get some useful life from it. The nice thing about a built-in modem is that it gets it power from the computer, freeing one space in your power outlet strip.

Back in olden times, when I first went on-line, my modem operated at a speed of 110 baud. (A "baud" is a measure of modem speed, roughly equivalent to bits per second. The name comes from J. M. E. Baudot, a pioneer in the field of digital communication.)

My 110 baud modem clacked along at a whopping rate of 10 characters per second. Since that time, I moved to 300 baud, then to 1200, 2400, and so on until getting my current 28.8 kb/sec modem. Each time I moved to a faster speed modem, I wondered how I ever survived with the slower one. Even today, I envy my friends who have dedicated high-speed connections to the Net, and wonder if we are finally getting to the speed limit for data pumped through analog phone lines.

My guess is that ways will be found to push even more speed through the copper wires in our homes. But, as you'll soon see, there are other inexpensive offerings on the horizon that will increase our bandwidth quite a bit.

But guess what? No matter how fast our communication lines operate, we will find ways to fill those pipes, leaving us screaming for "more bits!"

Speed thrills

Speed is important in modems for two reasons. First, a fast modem allows you to download documents faster than a slow one. While a 2400 baud modem might be adequate for plain text documents, it is painfully slow if you are trying to download graphics. And, it is totally inadequate for playing audio files or showing animation.

This brings us to the second reason that speed is important: A fast modem lets you do things you wouldn't think of doing with a slow connection to the Net. Because the Web has become a graphically-rich environment, anything slower than a 14.4 kb/sec connection will probably frustrate you beyond belief.

As a general rule of thumb, you'll find that a 14.4 kb/sec connection will limit you to AM-quality sound and small jerky video. Downloading anything more than text and small pictures at this speed is like trying to suck peanut butter up a soda straw.

Doubling the speed to 28.8 provides almost FM-quality audio. To do low-end video conferencing, you'll want to have an ISDN line operating at 128 kb/sec; and, for really high-quality audio and video, even faster lines are needed. Once you enter the realm of digital phone lines (such as ISDN, T1, and the other alphabet soup of offerings from your local telco), the price goes up — a lot! While ISDN pricing is fairly reasonable in most parts of the country (typically under $40 per month plus time and mileage), fast (megabit/sec) digital services can cost $2,000 or more per month. If we were limited to services at that price, the future of the Web would look bleak.

20

Fortunately, we are at the dawn of a bandwidth revolution that will reach into most businesses, schools, and homes. Data transfer speeds of 10 million bits/second are just around the corner. Most importantly, these fast data transfer speeds will be available at very low cost, insuring that this revolution will impact our homes and schools.

Before discussing some of the ways that the bottleneck of the voice-grade phone line will be broken, there is a caveat to share. A high speed line doesn't guarantee that the Web pages you seek will download instantaneously. A chain is only as strong as its weakest link. If you've been on the Web, you've probably noticed that sites that appear on your screen in a flash early in the morning may take forever to load in the middle of the day.

The Web is doubling in size every 90 days, and our telecommunications infrastructure is expanding as fast as possible, but gridlock hits the Web just as it hits our asphalt highways. Some popular sites (such as Netscape's home page, http://www.netscape.com) receive many million visits a day.

There are two ongoing developments that will help solve this problem. First, the capacity and speed of the Net's "backbone" is being improved all the time. Second, new strategies are being developed for compressing images, videos and sounds (all of which generally "hog" bandwidth). The combination of these parallel developments will make reliable and fast access to the Web a reality for all of us in the near future.

For whom the Bells toll...

While most of us currently connect to the Web through a voice-grade phone line, other alternatives are available, with new ones entering the market every month. There are a few developments in this area worth exploring.

@home

One of the exciting services that is preparing to launch in 1996 is the @home service (http://www.home.net/home2/home. html) operating over the television cable.

To understand this service, a bit of history is in order.

When cable TV first started, cable operators generally received television programming from a central source and then sent that information through the community to people's homes over copper cables. One of the problems with the use of copper was that the signal got weaker the further it traveled. To solve this problem, cable operators placed amplifiers along the cable route to boost the signal levels. These amplifiers required a connection to the power lines, and they were expensive to install and maintain. Furthermore, they only carried signals one way — from the central office to the home — and they were limited in the number of channels they could carry.

In order to save money, cable companies all over the country started switching to fiber optic communication lines to bring the signals to each neighborhood. The final connection to the home still uses copper, but the rest of the path is made of glass. There are several advantages in using glass fibers. First, the signals can be sent over very long distances without having to be re-amplified. Second, fiber optic lines have much higher bandwidth than copper cables, making it easy for cable providers to offer many more channels of programming.

The most exciting feature is that, with fiber optics, it is easy to provide a return path for communication from the home — something that is very expensive to do with the old copper-based systems.

Because most of the fiber's bandwidth is unused, all kinds of new services can be offered to homeowners at very low cost. One of these is high-speed access to the Net.

The @home service uses the television cable system for high-speed Net access. Users have to get a special converter box (about $300) to go between the TV cable and the computer's Ethernet port. Once connected, the @home service will provide access to the Web at speeds approaching 10 Mb/sec! The flat-rate fee for this service will probably be in the range of $30 per month for unlimited access.

As you can imagine, this might put a dent in the sale of $2,000 T1 lines to homes, but that's just the way technology is. Never a dull moment!

DirecPC

Don't have cable? All is not lost. If you've seen the new small DSS satellite dishes (they are about the size of a large serving tray), you've seen another tool for providing high-speed Web access. A service called DirecPC (http://www.direcpc.com) uses these dishes with a special converter to download Net-based information at speeds of about 144 kb/sec.

Because these dishes can only receive, not transmit, information, you might wonder how this can work. The key is that you initiate a connection along with your requests for information through your existing telephone line. Your request is then processed, and the resulting graphically rich data is beamed to your computer automatically through your satellite receiver.

The reason this works at all is because, for most of us, our Web usage is highly asymmetrical. We generally send mouse-clicks and typed text out to our Internet Service Provider (ISP), and receive color images, sounds and other rich media back. The channel from us to the ISP could be a lot smaller than the return path and we wouldn't notice it much. This will change dramatically when more of us start using the Web for video conferencing, but for now DirecPC offers some intriguing capabilities.

Intercasting

Have you ever watched a television program and wished you had instant access to in-depth information related to the show? Apparently enough demand exists for some television programs to have their own Web sites. During the '96 Olympics, avid fans had their televisions and computers on at the same time. While events were being broadcast, in-depth material was being posted to the Web.

A select group of viewers had a completely different experience, however. They watched the games on their *computer* monitors (using a special video card) and, without tying up a phone line, in-depth Web-based coverage of the games was downloaded to their computer's hard drive at the same time! Some of the people receiving these pages didn't even have accounts with an internet service provider!

So, how did they do it?

A new technology, called Intercasting (http://www.intercast. org), provides a way for related Web pages to be downloaded into your computer during the broadcast, for free.

The amazing thing about Intercasting is that it does not require a cable or telephone connection. You could be using an old rabbit ears antenna and, if you reception was good enough to see the TV show, you'll be getting the Web pages as well.

Here's how it works. Every television signal we receive in North America has 21 scan lines that are not seen. These lines are called the "vertical blanking interval," or "VBI." Several of these lines are used for closed captioning for the hearing impaired. Intercasting uses up to 10 of these lines to send Web documents. If you watch the program on your television set, it looks just like any other program. But, if you watch it on a specially equipped personal computer, in addition to seeing the TV show, the Web pages shipped over the VBI will be downloaded into your computer automatically.

The data transfer rate for this service ranges from 14 to about 96 kb/sec (depending on how many VBI lines are used), allowing a tremendous amount of information to be sent during a 30-minute or one hour program.

The downside of Intercasting is that there is no return path. Any links you click on with your mouse will be restricted to other materials that reside on your computer unless you also have a traditional Internet connection. In other words, Intercasting by itself is a completely asymmetric medium — it only sends information to you.

What do you need to receive Intercasting?

Your computer needs a special video card that not only receives television signals, but also is able to decode the information on the VBI. This one piece of hardware and one or two pieces of software might redefine television for the rest of the century!

Imagine the impact on education when educational videos can be accompanied by other resources, including simulation software, in-depth analyses, and references for further exploration. (For example, the science show, Nova, from WGBH (http://www.boston.com/wgbh/pages/nova/novahometxt.html) provides Intercast Web content.)

Intercasting is off to a good start. Intercast-ready computers started showing up in some computer stores in June, 1996. CNN provides Intercast content 24-hours a day, and NBC provided Intercast-versions of their Web pages during the '96 Olympic games.

Your Internet Service Provider

Proprietary services

Access to information on-line has been available for many years. A few years ago, interest surged as Prodigy, Compuserve and America Online (AOL) started offering access to e-mail and information sources for low hourly rates.

Two of the driving factors for the popularity of these services were ease of use, and the richness of their on-line libraries. America Online established a leadership position, even though it entered the market after Compuserve and Prodigy, largely because it offered a clean graphical user interface to its services.

Services of this type are called "proprietary" because they offer access to unique information sources. For example, AOL offers customers access to certain commercial publications, and the only way to get to this information is through a subscription to AOL's service.

For a long time, the only information that moved between services, or to the Internet itself, was e-mail. The proprietary services quickly discovered that, without offering global Internet-based e-mail, they would quickly lose subscribers to competing services that did offer this feature.

In the early 90's, pure Internet access from the home was generally secured through services that turned your personal computer into a text-based terminal providing access to telnet, gopher, ftp, and other services that required typing arcane commands. For many people, the power of a graphical user interface more than made up for the limited information found on the proprietary services, so AOL and its brethren continued to grow.

Then the Web took off as Mosaic brought the same point-and-click familiarity to the Net as a whole.

With Netarians at the gate, the proprietary services saw the writing on the hard drive: *Provide Internet access or die.*

Initially, services like AOL offered a weak graphical interface to traditionally text-based services like ftp and gopher, and this stemmed the tide for a while. But as the Web came to dominate the discussion, it became clear that any proprietary service that didn't also provide unlimited access to the Web would go out of business within a year.

Apple's e-World was the canary in the coal mine. This proprietary service never got a solid toe hold in the industry, and while Apple blinked, AOL and others offered Web access and e-World fell into oblivion.

Bill Gates initially announced that the fledgling Microsoft Network (MSN) would be a proprietary service and started signing up big names in entertainment and news to fill his hard drives. But just as he was getting ready to bring this service on-line, he re-read the tea leaves and wisely decided to make his a Web-based service. Fortunately only a few heavy hitters were left stranded at the MSN altar, when Brother Bill bobbed to the surface like bad cream in a cup of Java to announce that the Web was worth looking at after all.

Within a month, the press was almost ready to declare the Internet as yet another of Microsoft's inventions, much like the graphical user interface that my colleagues at Xerox PARC pre-emptorially stole from Apple and Microsoft several years prior to the formation of these companies. (And they say time can't run backwards!)

In any event, several proprietary services survive today simply because they also provide access to the Web. This should really be a cash cow for these providers, since they just have to pass the bits through their meters on their way to the Net without worrying about adding any value to the equation.

Should you sign up to the Web through one of these services?

It depends on your interests. If all you want is e-mail and Internet access, there are less-expensive choices available. If you also want access to some of the proprietary services that are not available any other way, then an account with AOL or another service might be a good choice.

Chances are, if you subscribe to any computer magazines, or have purchased any high-tech gear in the last year, you probably receive at least one floppy disk a week with the software needed to sign up to one of these proprietary services.

Traditional ISP's

In addition to the proprietary service providers, there are almost 3,000 companies that provide Internet access without any dedicated information repositories of their own. The purpose of these companies is to hook you to the Net through their gateways. Typically, they offer this service at a flat monthly fee of $19.95 or so (some are more, others are less). They typically provide the startup software you'll need, and that's about it.

In the olden days of the text-based Net when access was dominated by UNIX commands, these services were the domain of home-based wireheads. Now with the point-and-click ease of the Web, they are reaching a wider audience. The installation of the software is largely automated, and the services are easy to use. In fact, if you are content to just work with e-mail and Web browsing, these services are generally easier to use than the more full-featured ones like AOL.

Just about any magazine on computing or the Internet will have advertisements from ISP's. Most let you try their service for free. Since you'll be able to use virtually any Web browser you wish with these services, the differences between them will be based on three general criteria:

- Cost
- Local access
- Their ability to handle the traffic

Cost is specified up front, and is generally stated as a flat-rate fee.

If you are dialing in from home or from another location using a voice-grade phone line, you'll be dialing an access number. Clearly, you want this to be a local number so you don't run up toll charges. Any ISP will gladly tell you if your locality is served by a local call. If you travel a lot (as I do) you'll need to see if your service has local numbers in the various cities you are likely to visit. Many of these services also offer an 800 number, but they generally have an hourly surcharge for using this method of access.

Finally, you need to be assured that you'll get a connection when you want one. There is nothing more frustrating than dialing into one of these services only to be greeted by a busy signal. Alternatively, you might get logged on but find that your actual data transfer rate is way below the speed of your modem simply because the traffic on the service provider's lines is backed up.

Every ISP has been experiencing traffic jams, but you should inquire about their expansion plans and other strategies they have for insuring that you get the fastest access possible.

Who are the major players?

You can get an updated list of ISP's worldwide at http://thelist.iworld.com. If you want to start with some of the nationwide heavy-hitters, the current leader is Netcom (http://www.netcom.com). A recent report from CyberAtlas (http://www.cyberatlas.com) showed that in mid-1996 Netcom had 410,000 subscribers, followed by AT&T's WorldNet (http://www.worldnet.att.net) with 155,000 subscribers. AT&T is a recent entry to the ISP game, and their meteoric rise to the number two spot was based on a deluge of 600,000 inquiries received during their first few weeks of service.

There are many other fine service providers. In the period from April to June of 1996, the field grew by 42% bringing the number of ISP's worldwide up to 2,940.

Choosing a browser

A "browser" is a program that runs on your computer to facilitate your connection to the Web. Its function is to establish the connection to the Web page of your choice, to download special text files written in a language called HTML (Hypertext Markup Language) and to display these files as formatted documents on your screen. The first browsers supported text only (as did the Web itself a few years ago). Now, virtually all browsers support both text and graphics and, through additional "helper applications" and "plug-ins," you can explore Web pages containing sounds, movies, interactive multimedia applications, and even conduct video conferences.

One of the beauties of HTML is that it is platform independent. In other words, it doesn't matter if the computer you are using is a Macintosh, a UNIX machine, or one that runs Windows. The appearance of a page will be virtually the same on any computer you use and, if the creator of the site followed the HTML Standard, page appearance will be pretty much the same on any browser.

This also means that Web authors can develop pages on their machine of choice knowing that their handicraft will look as good on just about any computer someone has hooked to the Web.

Given the standardized nature of HTML, the choice of browsing software is up to you. While many browser programs support special features, most authors create pages using standard HTML code. This said, most of the browser-specific special features that are used are supported by Netscape Navigator. Because Netscape had about 70% of the browser market prior to Microsoft entering the field (Netscape's share grew to 84% shortly afterward according to Dataquest (http://www.dataquest.com)), Web authors are fairly safe in supporting this browser's special features.

Many of the browsers are free, at least for a trial period, so you should try a few to see which ones you like. Start with the one recommended by your Internet Service Provider. You can always switch to another one later.

A good list of browsers is maintained at http://www. browserwatch.com. In mid-June of 1996, this list contained information and links to over 60 programs!

Clearly you don't need to examine them all. I describe a few of the more popular or more interesting programs in the following sections.

Netscape Navigator

This product has maintained its strong lead by undergoing continuous refinement since it was introduced. Many of the features found on other browsers had their debut in this program. Because of its popularity, Netscape Navigator is packaged with the startup kits provided by many ISP's. Even if it isn't, you can purchase a copy, or download one from Netscape's site for free (http://home.netscape.com).

While you can download copies for free, business and home users are expected to pay a nominal fee (about $35) for the product. Educational users are not charged anything.

As this was written, Version 3.0 was the latest robust release. Beta versions of Navigator Gold were available as well. (The "Gold" version not only functions as a browser, but also lets you create Web pages of your own. We'll explore this topic in depth in a later chapter.)

Netscape quickly assumed a leadership role in helping to extend the capabilities of HTML, the language used to construct Web pages. In the beginning, Navigator supported text and images stored in the "GIF" format (more on this later). Support for JPEG images was added next, along with some extensions to HTML that allowed pages to have background colors and patterns, and for text to wrap around images.

Now the product supports tables, frames (several Web pages appearing in different windows on the same screen), JavaScript, Java, e-mail, support for third-party features called "plug-ins" and, soon, desktop conferencing.

It is clear from Netscape's direction that they intend for Navigator to be the major piece of software you'll need for all your network tasks.

Microsoft's Internet Explorer

While Netscape has the clear lead in browser software (according to Dataquest (http://www.dataquest.com), by the end of 1996 there will be more users of Netscape Navigator than of Windows 95), other vendors have excellent products worth examining. The current contender is Microsoft's Internet Explorer.

This software is available for free for all users from Microsoft's Web site (http://www.microsoft.com).

America Online chose this program as the browser bundled with its AOL service, and chose Netscape Navigator to bundle with its pure Internet service, GNN. This choice probably was influenced by Microsoft's willingness to bundle AOL with Windows 95.

Internet Explorer supports most of Netscape's features, including Netscape plug-ins, e-mail and Java. In addition, it has some nice features of its own. Musical files using the MIDI standard are sent directly to any synthesizer you have connected to your computer, and you can choose the display quality for pictures with a simple mouse-click. As should be expected, Internet Explorer also automatically handles Microsoft data types including WAV sound files and AVI movies.

One particularly nice feature is that type size on the screen can be increased or decreased using buttons along the top of the window, rather than having to use the Preferences settings as in Netscape Navigator. This is handy if you encounter a Web page using very small type, or if you are projecting a Web page on a screen to be seen by a large audience.

This product has a feature set that justifies its rapid rise to the number-two spot in the browser market.

Mosaic

Mosaic is the granddad of graphical Web browsers. This program resulted from Marc Andreesen's original work at the University of Illinois' National Center for Supercomputing Applications (NCSA), and it has undergone significant improvements since he left.

Prior to the release of Netscape, Mosaic had the number-one position in the Web browser market. Even though it has fallen from this position of dominance, it would be foolish to think that the brilliant programmers at NCSA are asleep at the wheel. It has continued to evolve and to incorporate new features.

Even though the underlying Mosaic technology has been licensed to commercial vendors like Spyglass (http://www.spyglass.com) and others, personal copies of the latest release of Mosaic can be downloaded for free from http://www.ncsa.uiuc.edu.

In addition to supporting Netscape-compatible plug-ins, Mosaic has several features of its own, including built-in capacity to read the text in Web documents out loud.

We'll have more to say later about projects at the University of Illinois (Mosaic's home) that may shape the Internet in the next decade. In the meantime, keep your eye on the folks who brought you Mosaic. Marc Andreesen isn't the only bright person who worked at the University of Illinois' NCSA.

HotJava

The HotJava browser from Sun Microsystems is written entirely in the Java language. We'll have more to say about Java later. For now, just know that Java is a language designed to allow the creation of Net-based applications which, when encountered, download for execution on your computer.

By creating the browsing program itself in this language, Sun has demonstrated the power of Java to create complex applications, as well as to provide some features lacking in current browsers.

The latest free release of HotJava can be found at http://java.sun.com.

While many of the features of HotJava are similar to those of Netscape Navigator, it does perform some tasks in uniquely nice ways. For example, several actions can take place at the same time. Multiple images load simultaneously, and you can start browsing immediately while images and Java applets are being loaded. Pages can be cloned so several windows can be open simultaneously without consuming any extra system resources.

Cyberdog

The Cyberdog (http://cyberdog.apple.com) system from Apple represents a radical departure from traditional browser designs. Cyberdog is a suite of interrelated programs that communicate with each other and the Net using the OpenDoc (http://opendoc.apple.com) technology developed by Apple, IBM, Novell, Oracle, WordPerfect, Taligent, and XSoft (a division of Xerox).

Here's how it works:

Instead of presenting a user with a monolithic application that supports third-party extensions (such as Netscape Navigator, or Adobe Photoshop), OpenDoc software provides the user

34

with a suite of smaller applications that work transparently with each other. Users can mix and match software modules to create a suite of tools called a "document." The various "parts" that form this document can be chosen by the user. This allows users to work in a task-centric rather than an application-centric manner.

Cyberdog is an OpenDoc document for Internet access containing several parts: a notebook, an integrated mail and news application, a Web browser and other tools you might want available as you explore the Net. Because the architecture of this environment is completely open, users can add functionality to Cyberdog by dragging new "parts" into the Cyberdog "document."

Nethopper

Imagine being able to surf the Web while riding the bus, or while sitting under a tree in the middle of a botanical preserve. This vision becomes reality if you have an Apple Newton 120 or 130 running a copy of Nethopper, a Newton-based browser from AllPen (http://www.allpen.com).

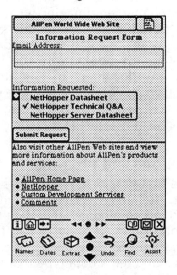

You can either use this product with a traditional modem connected to a phone line, or by using a wireless modem from Ricochet (http://www.ricochet.com). You can also hook a modem to some cellular phones and connect that way. Even more compact wireless modems from Megahertz (http://www.megahertz.com) and Motorola (http://www.motorola.com) will make wireless Web access commonplace in a year or two.

Because the Newton is currently limited to a black and white screen (no gray scale), most Web pictures look lousy on this display. For that reason, Nethopper uses text only. The result is quite acceptable for many informational sites, and this product hints at what the future might be like once the Newton becomes available with a color display screen.

The most exciting aspects of this product are access and price. You can purchase a Newton, a high-speed modem, and the NetHopper software for a combined price of about $800.

If your memory goes back far enough, you'll notice that this is not much more than what pocket calculators cost when they first appeared on the market. Imagine what the future will be like when small portable devices of this power become as commonplace as pocket calculators are today! Now, add to this a vision of wireless hookups to the Web that let you explore virtually any document in this huge informational space any time you wish, virtually anywhere you happen to be.

Nethopper brings this future just that much closer to today!

Helper applications and plug-ins

When Mosaic (the first graphical Web-browser) first appeared, it displayed text and images saved using the GIF format. Mosaic was able to accommodate other data types through the use of helper applications. If the user had these applications on the computer, then Mosaic would launch the appropriate one anytime it encountered a data type that was supported by the application.

For example, if a Web page had a link to a QuickTime movie, Mosaic would launch an appropriate movie viewer (*e.g.*, Simple Player on the Macintosh) and the movie would play in front of the Mosaic window.

This approach greatly extended the richness of media types that could be accommodated on the Web without requiring that the browser software know how to handle these data types itself. A downside to this approach is that the foreign data was displayed (or played) in its own window, not as part of the Web page that contained it. This led to clutter in some cases and, in any event, was an inelegant solution.

While helper applications are still used to some extent, a more popular approach today involves the use of "plug-ins" — applications that truly extend the functionality of the browser itself. This approach was started by Netscape and has since been incorporated in Microsoft's Internet Explorer. Microsoft (quite wisely) decided to support Netscape-compatible plug-ins rather than require developers to develop plug-ins for two incompatible platforms.

By themselves, most browsers today are pretty powerful. They can display text, graphics, programs written in Java and Javascript, and some limited forms of animation and sound. Plug-ins add so much functionality to the browser that the definition of what constitutes a Web document has been blown wide open.

The following chapter describes a few of the growing list of plug-ins available for your use. An updated list of plug-ins is maintained at http://www.browserwatch.com/plug-in.html.

37

What is the Web?

You may recall the old story of the blind men who encounter an elephant. When asked what it was, one man felt its tail and said it was like a rope. Another felt its trunk and said it was like a snake. Still another felt its leg and said it was like a tree, and so on.

By adding new features to Web browsers, plug-ins and helper applications allow us to expand our definition of the World Wide Web. Rather than think of the Web as a single medium, it is probably more productive to see the Web as a multi-faceted environment that is infinitely flexible, and becomes what we want it to be with a click of the mouse.

Let's explore a few facets of the Web:

The Web is a magazine

Most Web sites are informational. Since almost all Web browsers can display text and pictures right out of the box, virtually anyone with Web access can explore a wide variety of interesting magazines and newspapers, many of which are extensions of traditional print publications.

From a publisher's perspective, Web publishing has some advantages. Distribution is instantaneous, printing costs are zero, and search tools make it easy for readers to find articles of special interest to them. Links can be embedded in articles to let readers jump to in-depth background pieces that would not be of sufficient general interest to print.

Even though the page layout capabilities of HTML are limited, quite attractive layouts are still possible.

Some publishers want to preserve, as much as they can, the rich typographic possibilities of print-based publications. To serve this need, Adobe Systems (http://www.adobe.com) has created a plug-in to allow your browser to open and display files created in Adobe Acrobat. Acrobat files preserve detailed page layout, graphics and typeface information in documents that can be viewed and printed on any of the major computer platforms. The Acrobat plug-in supports "streaming." Streaming is a process by which the computer can start to display a file while it is being downloaded. Without this capability, you wouldn't be able to see, for example, the first page of a 100 page document until the entire document had been downloaded.

We use Acrobat files for many of our handouts at the Thornburg Center. They are compact, and they preserve the original layout.

How do publishers get paid?

Some Web-based magazines are available only to paid subscribers who have to type in a password in order to gain access.

For publishers who are willing to make their offerings available for free, some costs can be recovered through interactive advertisements scattered throughout the on-line "Webzine." This approach is used by Pathfinder (http://www.pathfinder.com), the home of the Time-family of publications (Time, People, Fortune, etc.)

Another strategy is to include information in the Web-based version that makes it complementary to the print version. The Web-version of MacUser (http://www.zdnet.com/macuser) contains shareware reviews that aren't in the print version, along with downloadable software. Subscribers to the printed version see the electronic format as an additional resource that makes their subscription even more valuable.

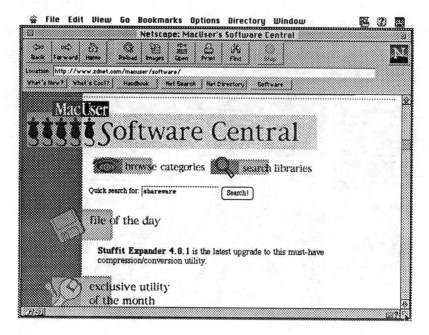

The low cost of entry makes it possible for special interest groups to publish their own magazines without having to incur the huge expense of printing and mailing.

From the user's perspective, "clippings" are easy to make since articles of interest can be saved to the user's hard disk for later reference.

A downside of Web-based publications is that they lack the portability and readability of the print versions. Established magazine publishers are likely to continue printing paper copies until we can purchase an inexpensive truly portable Web-based computer with the resolution and contrast of the printed page.

Lists of Webzines on a wide range of topics are maintained various places on the Web. One of the best lists is maintained at http://www.enews.com.

The Web is a radio

Radio is a powerful medium of expression. By adding audio playback capability to your Web browser, you can explore a variety of Internet radio stations (cybercast stations) that cover a much wider range of topics than most communities can offer over the airwaves.

Cybercast programs can be live, or archived for later playback. This archiving feature is quite valuable: It means you can listen to a program at your convenience, not just at the time it was broadcast.

From the perspective of the content creator, cybercasting has many advantages. First, the creator is freed from the tyranny of scheduled airtime. There are only 24 hours in a day, and every radio station has a pretty full schedule, so a new program is hard to schedule in most communities.

Second, sponsorship may not be needed if the program creator is willing to give the programs away. Alternatively, innovative sponsors may pay to get their message out on cybercast programs because their potential reach is huge.

Most communities have only a few dozen radio stations (limited by the AM and FM spectrum allocations). The reach of each station is typically under a hundred miles in radius. In the cybercast domain, there can be as many "stations" as Web sites, and each one can be accessed world-wide. The reach of this medium is truly global.

What are the drawbacks?

The main drawback today is sound quality, governed by the speed of your modem. Because (as of mid-1996) 67% of Web users have 14.4 kb/sec modems, cybercasters wishing to reach a large audience will optimize their content for this speed. The result is almost-AM-quality broadcasts that sound as if they were received on radios with small, cheap speakers.

43

While the playback quality improves markedly for content optimized for a 28.8 kb/sec modem, CD-quality sound is still some time off.

If you want to become a cybercaster (we'll show you exactly how to do this in a later chapter), you'll find the medium great for talk shows, but pretty poor for music.

For now, let's explore the tools you'll need to receive cybercast materials through your browser.

Tools

RealAudio

The main audio plug-in used today is RealAudio from Progressive Networks (http://www.realaudio.com). Because of its dominance in the market, you should download this plug-in first.

RealAudio supports streaming so you can listen to a file as it is downloading. Without this feature, live cybercasting would be impossible since you'd have to wait until the program was over and then download the entire audio file before playing it. (For those who prefer to listen off-line, some cybercasters let you download complete programs for playback at your convenience.)

If you've ever created audio files of your own, you know they take a lot of space. Our 15-minute cybercast show, *Perspectives on Education*, starts out at about 20 megabytes in size. The genius of Progressive Networks was in learning how to compress files of this size without totally destroying the quality of the audio signal. Our finished RealAudio files are well under one megabyte in size! This compact size is what makes it possible for these files to be played live over 14.4 kb/sec modems.

Even at this high level of compression (about 30:1), the result is quite acceptable for interviews and talk shows.

ToolVox

ToolVox by Voxware (http://www.voxware.com) is another popular tool for cybercasters. Unlike RealAudio, ToolVox is optimized for playing a single human voice. ToolVox files are quite small. For example, a 15-minute recording (17.6 MB, uncompressed) compresses to 801.5 kB with RealAudio at the 14.4 kb/sec setting. Using the ToolVox encoder, the resulting file is only 240 kB. This represents a compression ratio of over 73:1.

```
nerdy abbreviation alert
    M = mega (million)
    k = kilo (thousand)
    b = bits
    B = bytes
end nerdy abbreviation alert
```

You pay a price for this level of compression, however. The speech sounds much mushier than the corresponding RealAudio file, giving the speaker a slight lisp. I'd recommend sticking with RealAudio if you can.

ToolVox gets high points, however, for including a basic recorder with its free encoder software, so you can get up and running immediately. If space is at a premium, ToolVox may be worth the effort — especially if the original narration is crisp.

TrueSpeech

Like ToolVox, TrueSpeech (http://www.dspg.com) is also optimized for voice recordings. It supports high levels of compression with only moderate degradation in sound quality. Windows users can save sound files in the TrueSpeech format directly. Others need to convert to this special format using special software described at the TrueSpeech Web site listed above.

Content providers

You may still be wondering why anyone would want to listen to low-quality radio broadcasts on an expensive computer hogging space on the Net. Can you imagine families sitting around the living room computer listening to a modern equivalent of Mayor Laguardia reading the Sunday funnies?

Me neither.

This doesn't mean that cybercasting doesn't provide tremendous value.

First, let's consider the aspect of timing.

Most of us have VCR's to record television programs that are broadcast when we are busy doing other things. Not only can we play these tapes back at our leisure, we can build a personal library of videos to play whenever we wish.

For some strange reason, no one (to my knowledge) makes radios with built-in recorders that let you automatically record a program at some future time. As a result, there are lots of radio shows I want to hear, but miss because I don't have this tool. Through the medium of cybercasting, radio stations can build archives of their in-depth reports and other programs with long-term value that Web users can listen to whenever they wish.

Another feature of cybercasting is that it lets you hear programs from stations well outside their normal broadcast range. Travelers can hear the local news from home anywhere they have a connection to the Web if their hometown station has a cybercasting site.

And I've already mentioned that cybercasting makes it possible for anyone with interesting content to have their own "radio show."

Because (as with the Web in general) cybercasting is a rapidly growing medium, there are several Web sites designed to keep you updated on what is available.

Yahoo

The Internet search service, Yahoo, (http://www.yahoo.com/ Entertainment/Radio) maintains a list of net radio stations.

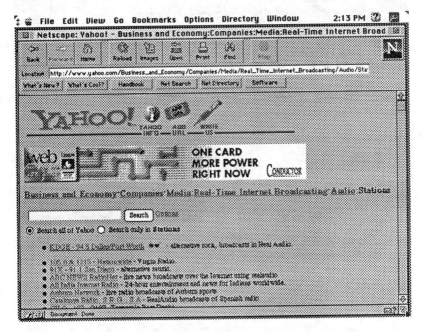

You can search for specific stations, or browse among the various selections. Many of the cybercast sites support more than one audio format, so you are likely to be able to hear programs without having to load any additional plug-ins.

TimeCast

Progressive Networks maintains a directory of cybercasting sites using the RealAudio technology. This site, http://www. timecast.com, is updated frequently.

An advantage of this listing is the ease with which you can choose the audio programming you wish to hear. Of course, since this site is sponsored by Progressive Networks, only RealAudio-compatible sites are listed.

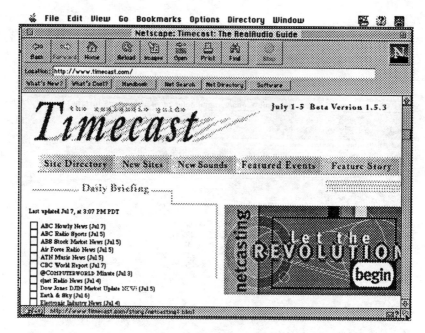

None of the reference sites provides an exhaustive list, however, so you should be on the lookout for audio content in any site that interests you.

The Web is a television

In the past few years we've all been inundated with hype regarding the convergence of computers and televisions. Set-top boxes promised to bring interactivity to millions of couch potatoes worldwide. Technologies like CD/TV, CD-I, and other elements of the alphabet soup of formats were going to turn the boob tube into a digital Einstein for the benefit of us all. We would have all our informational needs taken care of through the good graces of TCI and their kin. We could click ourselves to digital Nirvana with our remote controllers, dropping credit card numbers at appropriate inervals along the way.

That's not how it turned out. In fact, the concept of interactive television is an oxymoron — much like "airline food," or "military intelligence."

In the first place, the interlaced NTSC television screen is horrible for the presentation of text (As our associate Dr. Lynell Burmark asks, "Ever try reading movie credits on your TV set?") Second, when people sit six feet from a screen, the distance is too great to support personal interaction, but it is perfect for passive entertainment. Finally, the TV-set has the I.Q. of a water heater.

Computers, on the other hand, have a lot of intelligence, are designed with interactivity in mind, and can display high quality images and sounds. As George Gilder (http://www. discovery.org) says, the computer industry is converging with the television industry in the same sense that the automobile converged with the horse.

That said, computer- and Web-based television is in its infancy.

In July, 1996, Microsoft and NBC launched a new all-news television network with a linked Web page (http://www. msnbc.com). In addition to providing more in-depth news coverage than the traditional NBC offerings, the Web-site is synchronized so that interactive materials and background information are available at the time the TV show is being broadcast.

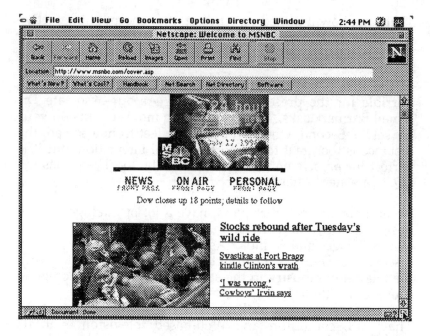

Today, MSNBC requires a hybrid approach — video delivered over the television set, and interactive materials delivered over the Web.

What about the future?

The idea of providing interactive television over the Internet is quite appealing. It probably has a great future, once broadband communication channels come into our homes. The problem is that, with today's modems operating over analog phone lines, video "Webcasting" reminds me of watching a dog walk on its hind legs: You are so impressed it can do it at all, you don't mind that it doesn't do it well.

Given that we can't even send CD-quality audio over the Web using traditional phone lines, and today's Web television is largely limited to postage-stamp-sized video playing back at a few frames per second, why bother?

The reason is that quality will improve as we learn more about pumping video over the Net, and we gain access to higher-bandwidth channels of communication. What you'll see on your browser today is only a hint of what's to come as the convergence of media continues to take place with our computers (and the Net) playing the central role.

Streamworks

Streamworks operates as a stand-alone video browser. After launching the free program (available from http://www. streamworks.com) you can choose from a menu of sites containing both live and pre-recorded video and audio programs. These programs are streamed to your computer, so they can be viewed while they are being sent.

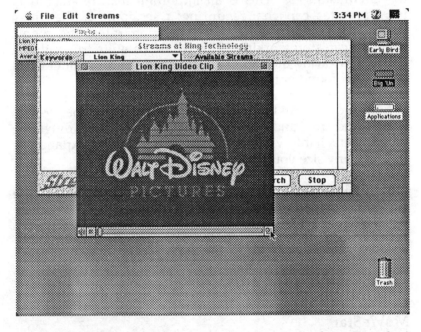

If you are using a dial-up connection (as most of us are today) the video quality is quite poor. This tool is no threat to television, yet.

When you give Streamworks a try, just remember what the original phonograph recording must have sounded like — and then note what you hear with today's audio CD's. The same revolution awaits Web television!

Vosaic

Researchers at the University of Illinois at Urbana-Champaign, the home of Mosaic, are in the process of bringing video to the Web with a Netscape-compatible plug-in called Vosaic (http://www.vosaic.com).

Vosaic's Video Datagram Protocol intelligently adapts to the available network bandwidth and processor power on your computer, providing the best possible video transmission under the circumstances. This is an important feature since data transfer rates can change during a session. If the video software can't adjust to these changing rates, the whole program can stop working. This would be quite frustrating if you were nearing the end of a movie and the browser crashed before you found out "who done it!"

A full set of control buttons in the Vosaic plug-in enables you to play and stop, and even fast forward or rewind through the video. Detachable video windows allow you to expand the image to any size you want.

Most interestingly, video hyperlinks embedded within the stream make objects within the video itself clickable — click on a video hyperlink to go off to another related page!

This product was not available for public demonstration at the time this chapter was written, but you should visit their site to get a copy when it comes out.

MovieStar

MovieStar (http://www.beingthere.com/moviestar) provides software for the creation and playback of Web-based QuickTime movies.

Once the MovieStar plug-in is installed in your browser's plug-ins folder (and QuickTime 2.1 or higher is installed on your system) you can navigate to sites containing pre-recorded as well as live video streams. Unlike StreamWorks, these videos show up on your browser's window just like an inset picture. MovieStar provides the typical QuickTime movie controls for adjusting sound volume, playing the video, fast forward, etc.

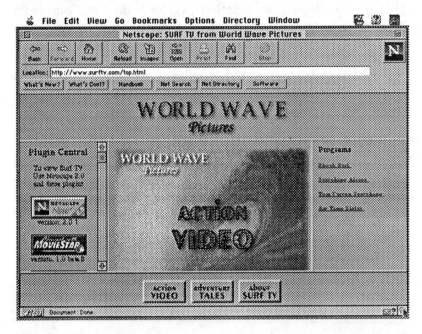

The playback quality over a voice-grade telephone line is not very good, but this product provides a taste of where Web-based video might head once the bandwidth issues are resolved.

MovieStar's site also provides a copy of MovieStar Maker, a full-featured video editing tool for creating your own streaming QuickTime movies.

QuickTime

QuickTime is the platform independent movie format developed by Apple, so you'd expect that they would have their own QuickTime plug-in available.

They do, and you'll find it at http://quicktime.apple.com.

This plug-in provides smoother playback than the one from MovieStar, but requires Netscape Navigator 3.0 to run.

As improved video tools appear on our computers, the line between Web browsing and television watching will start to blur for some users. It will be very interesting to see how this all plays out!

The Web is a presentation tool

As a public speaker, I conduct over 100 multimedia-based presentations each year. Since I generate all the content for these presentations myself, I've had to learn how to use a variety of image and sound editing tools, as well as master presentation tools like HyperStudio and Persuasion.

My presentations reside on my computer's hard disk or, increasingly, on separate 100 MB ZIP cartridges. When I arrive to give a presentation, I have a suitcase filled with the hardware and software I need.

There are many scenarios in business and education where this approach is not used, however.

Many presenters inside corporate offices give presentations in the field that were created by a resident staff. The person giving the presentation neither know nor care how to create multimedia. All they care about is insuring that the material being shared is accurate, attractive, and timely.

Consider the case where a sales force is dispersed throughout the country, giving presentations to clients in various cities. New information suddenly becomes available that must be included in the presentation. Traditional presentation tools require that the modified presentation be sent to every member of the sales team for installation on their computer. Given the travel schedule of many speakers (I average three time zones per week), the likelihood of the new presentation showing up in the presenter's city on time is often low.

If the entire presentation were located on the Web, then all the presenters would have immediate access to the same (updated) information.

While presentations can be created using traditional Web pages, most multimedia authors prefer to establish their own look and feel for presentations. Moreover, authors already familiar with tools like Persuasion, HyperStudio and Director, are understandably reluctant to take the time needed to master a new medium — especially one that is designed to be viewed by a single user rather than by a room full of people.

Several plug-ins and related tools have been created to alleviate this problem. These tools lend a new face to the Web. Their judicious use means that a presenter could conceivably show up at a client's office with nothing but a URL to the presentation Web site. Using the client's computer and projection system, a presentation can be made that looks the same on one platform as it does on any other.

Even if this capability is used only as a backup in case the presenter's computer fails, these Web-based tools are great assets to have.

The following sections describe a few of the plug-ins and related tools that just might change the way multimedia presentations are delivered.

Web Presenter

Adobe's (formerly, Aldus') Persuasion is a powerful tool for creating presentations. The basic structure of the program is an outlining tool that converts the outlines to a series of bullet charts for presentations. In addition to text, other media elements (images) can be incorporated. The presentation can be controlled with user-defined buttons that perform a variety of actions, such as moving from one slide to the next.

Presentations created with Persuasion can be fairly large — especially if they include graphics. This makes them awkward to post on Web sites since they would have to be completely downloaded before they could be seen.

Adobe has addressed this issue with the creation of Web Presenter (http://www.adobe.com), a prototype technology that provides some of the power and ease of use of Persuasion in a way that makes it appropriate for presentations to be delivered over the Web.

After creating a presentation in Web Presenter, the user can "print" it to an Acrobat 3.0 file. This highly-compressed document maintains all the interactivity of the original document: user-defined buttons work just as they should, for example. Furthermore, the slides become visible as the file is being downloaded, so you won't have to wait for the entire presentation to transfer to your computer before using it.

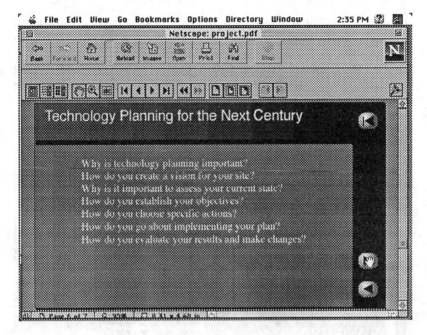

To view one of these presentations on your browser, all you need is the Acrobat "Amber" plug-in that can also be found at http://www.adobe.com. The versatility of this plug-in is so great that, if you don't already have it, you should install it in your plug-ins folder immediately!

HyperStudio

HyperStudio from Roger Wagner Publishing (http://www. hyperstudio.com) is a premiere multimedia creation tool that provides much richer functionality that outline-based tools like Persuasion. This is the tool I use in virtually all of my multimedia presentations.

Most of my HyperStudio presentations are quite large, and are impractical to post on the Web, especially for access by people using ordinary telephone line access to the Net.

This problem has been partially alleviated by the creation of a HyperStudio plug-in (http://www.hyperstudio.com/lab/

plugin.htm) that works in conjunction with a free HyperStudio player application to let you interact with multimedia documents and presentations that have been posted on the Web. Web-based HyperStudio projects can contain a rich assortment of media — images, sounds, and QuickTime movies, to name a few.

Unlike Web Presenter, the HyperStudio plug-in does not support streaming. This means that the entire file must be downloaded before it can be seen. Successful authors will see this as a challenge to keep their files compact — a good practice in general when posting anything to the Web!

Other plug-ins for presentation packages are being released on a regular basis. Be sure to visit the plug-in library at http://www.browserwatch.com/plug-in.html for the latest information.

The Web is a telephone

Voice communication over distance has enthralled many of us since we first learned to stretch a string between two tin cans and whisper messages to someone 20 feet away. Citizen's band radio brought the tin cans into the electronic age, allowing us to chat up a storm with complete strangers! And — no surprise here — one of the most controversial topics surrounding the Web today has been the use of this medium to place long-distance phone calls — for free.

Through use of the appropriate plug-in or stand-alone application, two-way voice communication is possible anywhere in the world the Internet exists.

Many telephone companies are having cardiac arrest at the prospect that people will bypass their meters. As with cybercasting, the voice quality leaves a lot to be desired (even at 28.8 kb/sec) but the telcos are smart enough to realize that this is a temporary problem.

Several of them launched petitions to outlaw "netphones," although their reasoning is generally limited to a convoluted attempt to avoid the truth: They are ticked off because some enterprising entrepreneurs saw an opportunity the huge telcos had missed. After all, if they feel that all long-distance voice communication should run through them, why haven't they tried to shut down Amateur Radio?

AT&T is one of the few actually embracing the concept, and who thus has a chance to make some money at it while the other Bells were sniping at the highly scattered brotherhood of Web users.

This battle is so much fun to watch that you'll want to explore netphones yourself just to see what the fuss is all about. Updates on this conflict are maintained by the Voice on Net coalition, located at http://www.von.org.

VocalTec Internet Phone

How does an Internet phone work? It isn't just a matter of getting a dial tone and pushing a few buttons. VocalTec's Internet Phone (http://www.vocaltec.com) provides an address book listing a series of chat rooms you can join for a conversation. If you want to have a private conversation, you can set up a private chat room which is "unlisted." This way you can give the name of this room to the person you wish to talk with and know that your conversation will be moderately private.

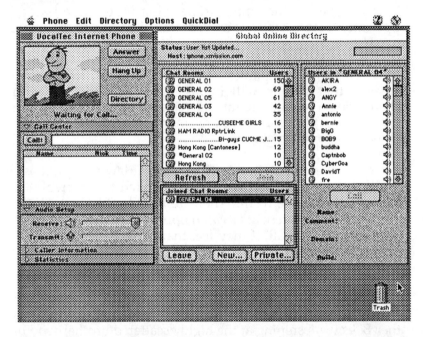

Alternatively, you can enter the address of your party's Internet site and connect directly that way. Of course, the Internet Phone software has to be running on your contact's machine in order for this to work.

Once you are connected, the process is pretty easy. If you are using the Macintosh version of the software, the result is like a normal phone call where you can listen and talk at the same time. On computers that do not support "full-duplex," the experience is more like CB-radio — you each have to speak in turn.

PGPfone

PGPfone (http://web.mit.edu/network/pgpfone) provides voice communication with an additional feature. It not only makes phone calls over the Net, it insures that the call is secure through the use of the PGP encryption algorithm.

If you've followed the world of network communications in the past year or so, you've probably come across the name of Philip Zimmerman — the creator of PGP (Pretty Good Privacy). His creation and subsequent free distribution of "strong" (hard to break) encryption for e-mail and other files resulted in a protracted fight with governmental agencies who thought that privacy was great, as long as they held the keys. The PGPfone manual provides a great history of this battle and is worth reading, even if you never use the free product!

As of this writing, PGP is fine for use in the United States, but generally not for export to other countries. The privacy advocates staged a noble defense of Zimmerman's activities, and this encryption technology has now been applied to Net telephony through PGPfone.

Clearly the function of this product is quite different from that of VocalTec's Internet Phone. You'll be contacting the receiving party directly rather than going through a public "chat" room.

If you want a private conversation, PGPfone should give it to you.

As Brad Templeton of Clarinet once said, "When cryptography is outlawed, bayl bhgynjf jvyy unir cevinpl!"

The Web is a conference center

As originally envisioned, the Web was a place for the posting, retrieval, and linking of documents. As the previous sections have shown, it is now becoming much more than that.

One of the more exciting developments is the use of the Web (and the Net in general) as a vehicle for collaboration and interaction. Net-based telephones provide some capabilities in this area, but even more powerful tools let you take part in interactive conferences where users can communicate with each other, transfer documents as easily as handing them across a table, and draw pictures or make markups on a shared document workspace.

Traditional video conferencing provides two-way video and audio using very expensive equipment and high-speed (ISDN or better) phone lines.

The growing field of desktop video conferencing is just starting to emerge. Rather than requiring specialized hardware and communication lines, desktop conferencing uses your personal computer and, in some cases, works quite well over existing voice-grade phone lines.

As for the cost, some conferencing packages are available for free.

The quality of desktop conferencing is not as high as that provided by dedicated equipment — yet. This will change.

Before exploring a few of the kinds of tools that are available, think about the tremendous opportunities that real-time desktop conferencing could bring to your school or community! Meetings could be scheduled with participants located all over the country, each of whom would be able to take part in the conference for (in many cases) the cost of a local phone call.

I fly across the country almost weekly, giving presentations at conferences and consulting with clients. Many of the people seated next to me on the airplane are flying across the country to take part in a one- or two-hour meeting.

There is no question in my mind that desktop conferencing will have a tremendous impact on these folks when they realize that they can accomplish as much from their home base without wasting a day in travel. Of course, this will also have an impact on the airline industry as these full-fare business flyers decide to move information, not atoms!

Here are a few Web and Net-based conferencing tools that are worth exploring:

CU-SeeMe

CU-SeeMe (http://www.wpine.com/ins.htm) started out as a free video conferencing tool created at Cornell University (CU). It originally allowed black and white video images to be sent over the Net from one user to another or, through the use of a reflector site, for several participants to take part in the same conference.

Now that the product is being commercialized (a free thirty-day trial version can be obtained from the site listed above), new features have been added. Audio conferencing is built-in, as is a shared canvas for participants to use for working in a common graphical space.

This product is almost too feature-laden to use over a 28.8 kb/sec modem. Images take a long time to refresh, making the video hard to use, and speech breaks up as well!

If you have access to higher speed connections, CU-SeeMe is a powerful product with a very reasonable price. At current dial-up data rates, this product demands too much from your connection to be useful.

It is worth looking at, though, because CU-SeeMe was (so far as I know) the first tool designed to support videoconferencing over the Net. For that reason alone, you should try a copy.

Netscape Chat

At the opposite extreme, Netscape's Chat 2.0 (http://www.netscape.com) provides a basic text-based chatting tool for typed dialog with users who join a conference room.

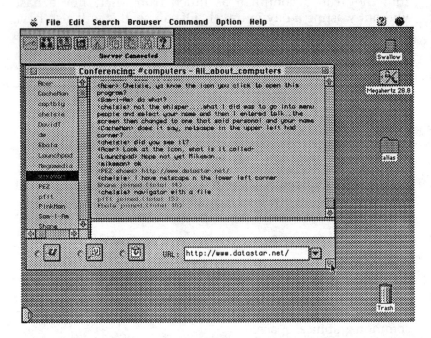

This free product extends the capabilities of Netscape 2.0 to support conferencing. Because the messages consist of text, this product works beautifully on dial-up connections to the Net. Chat 2.0 is just one indicator that Netscape sees its browser as more than a Web tool. It forms the foundation for virtually all of the activities you might want to take part in on the Internet.

Roundtable

Roundtable from the Forefront Group (http://www.ffg.com) is a useful conferencing tool for those of us with dial-up Net access. This free product works as a helper application for your browser. When you launch the program, you can access an address book listing various conference rooms at Forefront's site. You can choose to join an existing conference, or can select users and establish a private conference of your own.

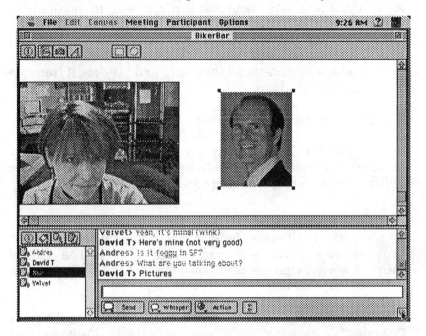

Conferences can also be established at any other Web site that has purchased the Roundtable server software.

Once you are connected, you'll have a canvas that can be seen by everyone in the conference, as well as a text window for typing and receiving messages from conference participants. Roundtable supports still images in color, as well as text-based messages, so the product works well on low-bandwidth phone lines.

Even though this product lacks the glamour of some videoconferencing tools, it more than makes up for this limitation through a rich set of features. For example, if you find it distracting to move your eyes from the shared canvas to the text windows, you can assign different synthesized voices to each of the participants and their messages will be read to you when they are received.

Also, if you have any document that you wish to distribute to members of the conference, all you need to do is drag the document icon from your desktop to the canvas window, and it will appear on each recipient's screen. If they want to download the document, all they have to do is drag it from the canvas to their desktop.

It doesn't get any easier than that!

By designing a product designed to take advantage of low-bandwidth connections, Forefront has provided Web users with a very useful conferencing tool.

The Palace

A completely different twist on conferencing software is provided by a Time-Warner venture called The Palace (http://www.thepalace.com) through a suite of shareware software applications.

The Palace is an outgrowth of MUD's, or "Multi-User Domains" — basically chat rooms with context. Ordinary chat tools (such as Netscape's Chat) allow conference participants to type messages to each other. The Palace extends this metaphor by providing a visual space for the interaction, with each conference participant having a unique visual identity. The background can be anything the host desires.

For example, Appleby's Digital Imaging (http://home.apete. nb.ca) has created a photo-replica of the historical city of St. Johns, New Brunswick you can visit.

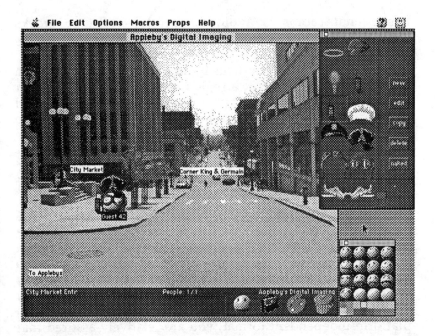

(I'm the happy face with the cell phone.)

Visitors to this virtual city can travel along the streets, enter buildings, and engage in dialog with other visitors who may happen by.

The modest $25 shareware fee for The Palace allows you to create a unique visual representation of yourself (your "avatar"), as well a letting you create complete virtual worlds of your own.

Once you have created your own Palace, you can mount it on your Web site for others to visit.

Aside from recreational applications, this product has many other uses. Imagine a conference in which participants can "seat" themselves around a conference table while they engage in a dialog. Because each participant can be represented by his or her digitized photograph, the relative anonymity of text-based chat rooms is avoided, yet this software works splendidly over voice-grade telephone lines.

Educators might have students build a virtual world based on a book they have read, or a region they have studied. Other students could then visit these virtual worlds and engage in dialog with their peers to demonstrate their mastery of the subject represented by the setting.

The Web is interactive software

Java

Of all the hype surrounding the Web, my guess is that none has generated as much press as the release of Java. Java is a programming language developed by some of the geniuses at Sun Microsystems (http://java.sun.com). Its function is to allow compact programs (called "applets") to be sent from a Web site to your computer where they can be run directly by your browser. Because each applet is compiled to a special platform-independent format, you are relatively assured that Java programs will run similarly on any computer you happen to be using, as long as you use a browser that is "Java aware."

This is a completely different model from the time-sharing programs you might have experienced if you were involved with remote computing in the 1960's. (Yep, by cracky, them wuz the days!) With Java, the program sails over the Net to your machine where it does its stuff.

Sun is promoting the idea that, with the proper suite of Java applets, you'll be able to create complex database management programs, or word processors, or just about anything else you are currently buying shrink-wrapped software to accomplish. Unlike today's bloatware with 20-disk installs, you simply assemble the elements you need for your particular task, and (if the supplier wants to charge you), you only pay for the features you need.

This is an intriguing idea. So intriguing, in fact, that Java programming workshops fill up within days of their announcement.

Before you rush out to learn Java, you'll want to get your C++ chops in order, since Java is based on this language. (Technically, Java should be called C++--, since it has many of the features of C++, without the ability to easily create viruses or other programs that can wreak havoc with Web sites or your computer.)

If Java programming isn't your cup of tea (now THERE is a strained metaphor for you!) you can still see what all the excitement is about by exploring some of the applets created by others.

One of the best libraries of Java applets can be found at http://www.gamelan.com. This site is updated on a regular basis, and you can play with the programs others have created to your heart's content.

At this stage of development, Java is in its infancy. You'll be able to see enough at the Gamelan site to understand why this development is important.

Considering the Web's humble origins, Java highlights the incredible developments that have taken place in a very short period of time.

You might be so excited by what you see that you want to create some animated interactive doodads of your own. What then?

Fear not.

Interactive Web animation tools exist for those of us who think a subroutine is the work schedule for someone at a sandwich shop.

Web Animator

One of the more elegant of these is Web Animator from Deltapoint (http://www.deltapoint.com). This suite of software consists of an authoring tool for creating interactive animations of your own, and a Netscape-compatible plug-in to allow these animations to be played back when you encounter them on the Web.

The authoring software lets you create a series of key frames. Graphical elements can be created within the software, or you can paste in graphical objects created with other tools.

Transitions between these frames (including the movement of objects) are then computed on the fly as the animation plays back. This keeps the resulting files quite small. Web Animator supports streaming, so your files start playing as they are loading onto your computer.

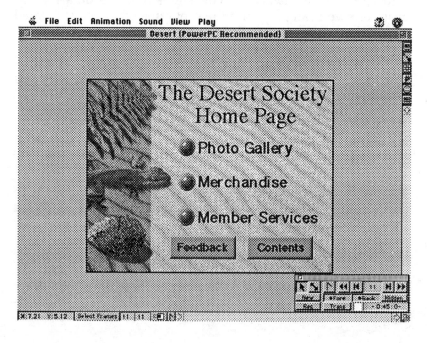

When designing your animations, most of your creative work is done by manipulating the graphical objects themselves, keeping the process as intuitive as possible. Storyboard views of your keyframes provide an easy way to structure your projects.

One of the stellar features of Web Animator is its extensive use of AppleGuide, an interactive help system that shows you, step by step, how to perform virtually any task you want! This all but eliminates the need for a manual!

CelAnimator

Another powerful authoring tool to create and edit animations for the Web, is CelAnimator from FutureWave (http://www. futurewave.com).

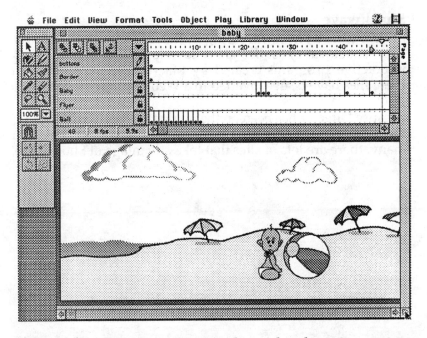

Like Web Animator, this product also lets you create interactive animations without having to become a programmer. It has a very rich feature set and creates files that can be run on your browser using a compact Netscape-compatible plug-in called FutureSplash.

By using vector graphics, CelAnimator files are quite compact, and start playing as they are loading. Users who encounter these files during their browsing don't have to wait very long to start interacting with the software.

CelAnimator files can be converted to special animation files (called "gif'89" files), but, as of this writing, the results are not as good as using the plug-in. The one advantage of gif'89 files is that they play back on most browsers without requiring any plug-ins. We'll describe this technology (and point you to some more tools) in a later chapter.

Shockwave

Macromedia's Shockwave plug-in (http://www.macromedia. com/shockwave) is designed to allow you to play back interactive programs created by Macromind Director, after these files have been converted to a Web-appropriate format.

Because Director has been on the market for many years, and is the industrial-strength multimedia authoring tool of choice for many, there are lots of sites that take advantage of Shockwave.

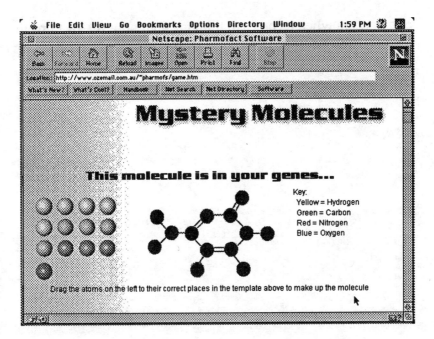

If you are just starting out, you should know that Director requires years to master, and is the subject of semester-long courses at many community colleges. If you are going to put that much effort into learning something new, you might as well learn Java.

If, like me, you are interested in tools that fit well into a lifestyle that involves more than staring at a computer screen all day, then stick with the other tools I mentioned for your own creations.

The Web is ???

The Web is many things today, and it promises to become many more tomorrow. It is as if this environment were an infinitely flexible environment. The Web is limited only by the human imagination.

It is little wonder that the Web has generated so much excitement in the past year or so. We are clearly at the dawn of a new era when it comes to thinking about our interactions in the rich informational space of the Internet.

Browsing vs. Searching

The previous chapters have listed many interesting Web sites — places to visit for information or software. There are lots of books on the market that contain lists of sites covering a wide range of topics. These books are filled with great information, but they all suffer from the same problems that plague this one.

- The information they list may be out of date by the time you read it.

- New information of interest to you will surely have been posted on the Web in the previous 24 hours.

- The information listed in books (or magazines) might point you to sites in your general interest areas, but leave you with the nagging feeling that even better sources of information are out there, if you just knew how to find them.

The generic Internet joke goes like this: The Internet is the largest library in the world, but it has no card catalog.

Well, actually, that isn't a joke, is it?

Look at the metaphors we use for exploring the Web, "browsing" or "surfing" top the list. Imagine you were doing a research project at your local library. Would you be content to just browse among the thousands of volumes present? Imagine your library's collection doubling every 90 days! Browsing wouldn't work in a physical library, and it would be even more futile to try this approach in the virtually infinite library comprising the Web.

Instead of surfing along predefined informational domains with a series of mouse clicks, we need to be able to go fishing in the depths of the Web. Fortunately, there are plenty of tools to help us in this task.

We'll explore two classes of tools in this chapter. The first are designed to help you find the information you are looking for, and the second are designed to help you organize and keep track of this information once you've found it. Mastery of these two skills, more than any others, will turn the Web into one of the most powerful tools at your disposal.

Search tools

The Web hosts quite a few sites whose primary job is to let you conduct searches for information. Before exploring some of these sites, let's examine some of the general strategies that apply to them all.

First, you need to have a good idea what you are looking for. Suppose you are looking for information on purchasing a car. You might ask these search tools to give you all the information they can find on cars.

Imagine what you'd get in response. Sure, you'd get information on automobiles. You'd also get information on railroad cars, antique cars, and a general list of every Web site that has the word "car" in it.

Clearly, "car" is too broad a category to be useful.

You can also err on the other side by phrasing your search criteria so tightly that you miss some of the Web sites that you'd like to know about. Most search engines are not very smart. You can't say, "You know what I mean..." Most of these sites only work with the words you give them.

Fortunately, with a little practice and experience with several search engines, you'll find a few that fit your personal style and that get you the information you want. We'll explore this a bit when we describe some of the search tools.

How do the search tools work?

When a new Web site is created, the creator sends a message to the various search pages announcing the location of the new site. Within a day or so, the various search engines visit the site and build an index of its contents. This index is updated periodically so the search tools provide as up-to-date a listing as possible. During the Net's "slow" periods, the various search engines prowl through the Web looking for new information that may have been added since the last index was built.

When you use one of these sites to locate information, it searches through its own index. This means that the information may not be completely up to date. Also, some of the indexes may have information from sites that haven't been listed with other search tools. For this reason, you may find yourself using a few of these search tools on a regular basis, especially if you are looking for obscure information.

Again, the best way to tell which tool to use is to try them all and stick with the ones that give you the best responses.

Yahoo

Yahoo (http://www.yahoo.com), one of the first Web indexes, was started in 1994 by Jerry Yang and David Filo, two Stanford graduate students. As with other Internet-based companies, its stock sailed into the stratosphere when the company went public. With a personal net worth of over $100 million, Jerry is probably not too distressed that he dropped out of grad school to work on this project.

Yahoo provides two things of value — a method for searching the Web for information, and a list of Web sites arranged by categories that you can search through, or browse to your heart's content. As with the other services, Yahoo's library grows daily.

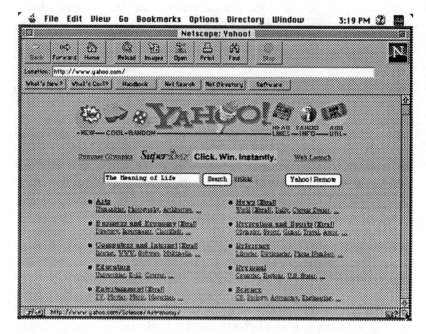

As a user, you are provided with a text window for typing the words or phrase you want to use in your search. (For the rest of this chapter, we'll search for the Meaning of Life.) Once this request is typed in, a simple mouse click on the Yahoo's search button initiates an examination of their entire database. Web sites that contain the desired words or phrases are then listed on a fresh page in the form of hypertext links. They are arranged by rank, with those having the closest match to your request being listed before those where only a portion of your request is matched.

To visit any of these sites, you just click on its link and your browser will take you there directly.

WebCrawler

WebCrawler (http://www.webcrawler.com) is one of the easiest search engines to use. Just type in your request and wait for the responses.

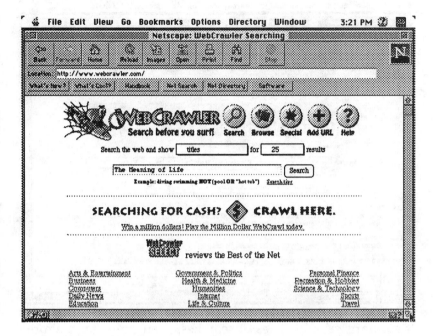

As with Yahoo and some of the other services, WebCrawler provides subcategories you can browse. It also lets you search backwards to find sites that reference a particular site of interest. For example, I can easily find a list of people who have created links to the Thornburg Center (http://www.tcpd.org) on their Web site. This feature is included with other search services as well, but the interface in WebCrawler is quite nicely done.

WebCrawler also provides a lot of information about the growth of the Web, and this portion of the site is worth examining by itself.

AltaVista

AltaVista (http://altavista.digital.com) is an incredibly powerful search environment created by Digital Equipment Corporation.

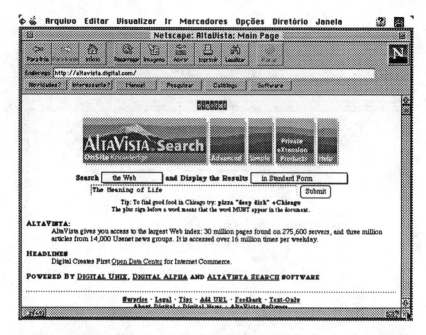

It supports several types of searches. You can enter a simple phrase or series of words or, if this doesn't give you the right results, you can formulate your request using Boolean logic (with a few twists). Using their advanced search feature, you could ask for all the sites listing Dole AND Republican NOT pineapple, for example.

Which reminds me of the Logic joke in which a fellow calls his insurance company: "My house was burglarized!" "No problem," said the agent, "Did it also burn down?" "No, it was burglarized, that's all." "Sorry," the agent replied, "but we can't help you. It seems you were insured for fire AND theft; you should have had fire OR theft."

OK, so this is why there are so few logic jokes.

Infoseek

Infoseek (http://www.infoseek.com) provides a sophisticated site with many features.

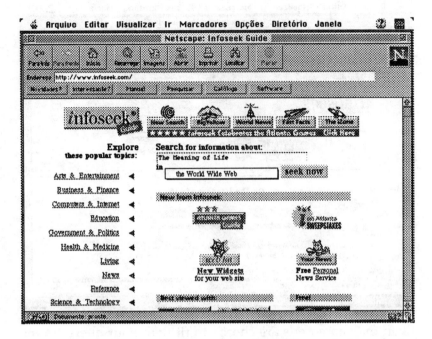

Requests can be entered in plain English, and the results appear in two places: first, you'll get a list of specific citations (as with the other search engines), and, in the left column, a listing of general categories that might relate to your search.

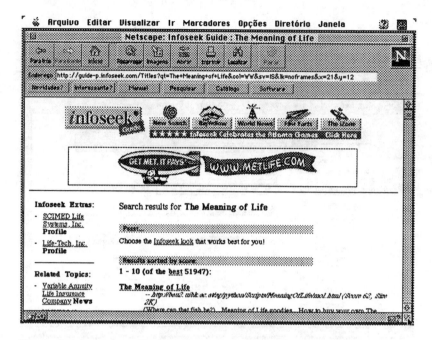

Even the banner ads are chosen to fit with your query (to the extent possible.

Subsets of the search can be found with a single mouse click for those responses containing the words "similar pages." As with Yahoo, Infoseek also supports browsing by subject.

For those who are creating their own Web pages, Infoseek provides the capacity for you to add links to some of their custom services (*e.g.*, stock quotations) for free.

Lycos

The Lycos site (http://www.lycos.com) supports browsing by subject as well as a full set of Web searching tools. Your search is automatically expanded to include related words. For example, The Meaning of Life request was expanded to include the following words: "meaning," "meaningful," "life," "lifestyle," and "lifetime."

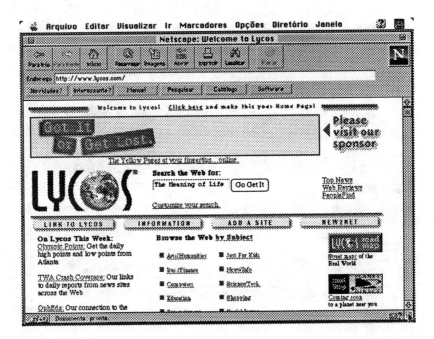

Its features are similar to those of the other tools.

As I said before, none of these tools has mapped the entire Web, so you'll probably want to use several when conducting your search to get as complete a list of relevant sites as possible.

Search.com

One of the more interesting tools is the Search.com site from c|net (http://www.search.com). It provides your choice of search engines all from one central location. If you use several search tools on a regular basis, you'll probably want to use this central site to launch your searches.

It supports full Web searches as well as express searches which only examine a hand-picked subset of the Net. You can choose the search engine for any of these, as well as do a search within a specific subject area (*e.g.*, Education).

One unique free feature is the ability of Search.com to create a personalized search page just for your interests. Once you've filled out the forms needed to choose the search tools you want, Search.com creates a custom page (with up to 20 search engines listed) that you can use by clicking on "Your page" from their main screen!

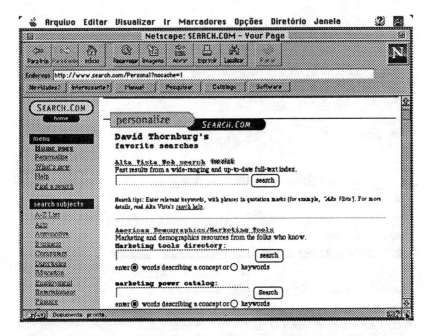

Once you've created your custom page, Search.com will recognize you when you log on and give you the chance to go there for your searching.

Shareware.com

So far, all the tools I've mentioned are geared to general information.

Suppose you are looking for software — specifically for shareware or freeware. One of the best tools for finding software can be found at Shareware.com (http://www. shareware.com). This search engine, maintained by c I net, has a fairly thorough listing of software archived at sites all over the world. Software can be searched by platform. It doesn't matter if you are want a Macintosh, DOS, Windows, UNIX, Amiga, Atari or other program, If you know what you are looking for, you can just enter its name, and, in a few seconds, a list will appear showing the sites that have this program available for downloading.

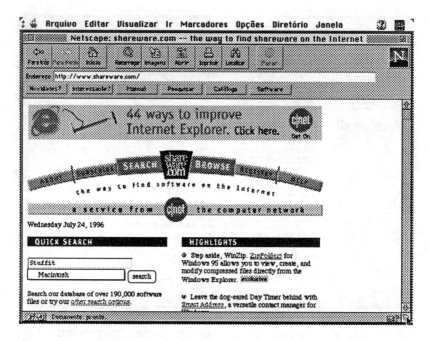

One of the features of this tool is that the resulting list is indexed by the speed and reliability of the download site so the actual transfer goes as smoothly as possible.

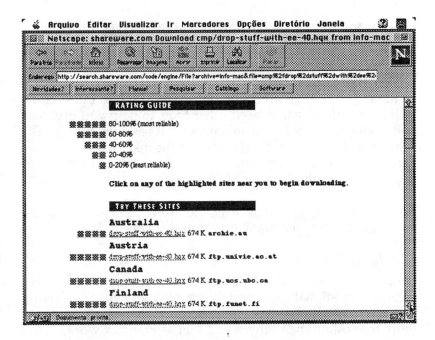

To download a program to your computer, you just have to click on the site you want to use, and the software will be transferred to your machine. Usually, these files are first compressed and then converted to a special format so they can be transmitted easily over the Net. Once these files get into your computer, your browser will automatically launch the decompression software needed to convert them back into the form your computer needs in order to run them. (You must have this file expansion software on your computer, but it is almost always included with the startup kit from your ISP).

You'll find yourself building a great software library quite quickly. Just be aware of two things:

- After your software has been decompressed, let your anti-virus software have a peek at it to be sure it is clean.

- If you've loaded a "shareware" program that you plan to use on a regular basis, be sure to send in your registration fee. This is not only ethical, it also provides incentives for

87

the author to keep the program up-to-date, and to provide even more great products in the future!

Other tools

While search engines are great for helping you find information in the first place, you'll need other tools to help you organize and keep track of this information after it has been found. The following descriptions typify some of the many tools available to serious Web-users who are counting on the Web to meet their professional or academic research needs.

As with many of our other lists, the products below are just a small sampling of the many fine tools available today.

Net Ninja

Sometimes I just sit at the computer clicking my way through some informational space and the next thing I know I'm having a ball in some site I've never seen before. Some of my paths are more interesting than others, and I let serendipity work on my behalf.

The problem is that, a day after I've logged off, I suddenly realize that one of the sites I got to by accident had some wonderful content, but I can't remember its name!

Net Ninja (available from http://www.zdnet.com/macuser/ utility.html) automatically builds an index of every site you visit. You don't even know the program is working for you since it does all of its work in the background. There have been several occasions when I've been thrilled that this tool was building a collection of URL's for me.

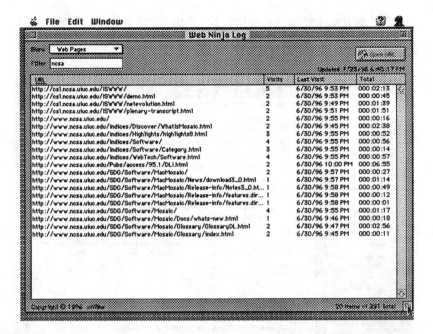

Sites you've visited are kept in a list you can refine and scroll through at any time. This list can get quite huge because Net Ninja keeps a record of every single page you visit. Fortunately, you can restrict the display by typing in a element that is common to all the site addresses you're interested in. For example, entering "ncsa" will display the names of any sites you've visited with "ncsa" anywhere in the site's name.

Once you've found the site you're looking for, you can select it an have Net Ninja take you there by automatically launching your browser.

WebArranger

WebArranger (http://www.cesoft.com) is so powerful, it is the main program I use on my laptop.

On the surface, WebArranger is an outliner for the capture and organization of ideas. Because outline elements can be expanded into text windows, this tool can be used to expand text in some depth. (The first draft of this book was written in WebArranger, for example.)

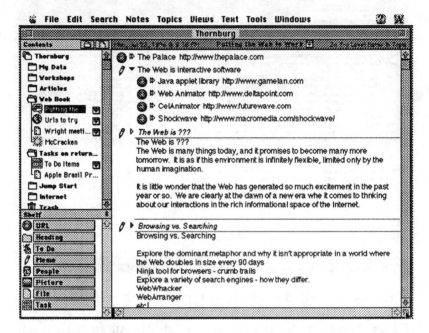

While outliners are nothing new, WebArranger has a few other features that make it interesting. Individual notes can have any of several characteristics. They can be text, dates calendar entries, pictures, personal contact lists or even addresses to Web sites. Each of these object types has different features and capabilities.

The Web-site type (called URL) lets you enter a Web address along with a description of the site. If you wish to visit the site, all you then need to do is select its entry within your document and, with a single command, WebArranger will launch your chosen browser program, log you onto the Net (if you aren't on-line already) and take you to the site.

WebArranger has many other capabilities, but this feature alone makes it indispensable in my work.

Like Net Ninja, WebArranger also lets you maintain a history of all the Web sites you've visited, increasing the utility of this tool even more.

When you purchase your copy of WebArranger, you'll even get a free copy of another fantastic program, WebWhacker.

WebWhacker

Every so often you'll encounter a site so fantastic and useful that you'll want a copy of the entire Web site on your hard drive so you can explore it anytime you wish, even if you aren't hooked up to the Web.

While every browser provides some limited capacity to save Web pages as HTML files, pictures and other media elements are not saved with the HTML document. This is fine for text-only sites, but many of the interesting sites have graphs and pictures that are essential elements of the information you want to keep.

WebWhacker (http://www.ffg.com) lets you choose a Web site for downloading. After specifying how many levels down you wish to go, you set WebWhacker to work in the background, and the entire site (if you've chosen that option) will be transferred to your computer where you can explore it to your heart's content. This means that all the text, pictures and other media elements are saved in a place of your choosing and are then linked together so the resulting hard-disk version accurately mirrors the one you'd see on-line. (Not surprisingly, these are called "mirrored" sites.)

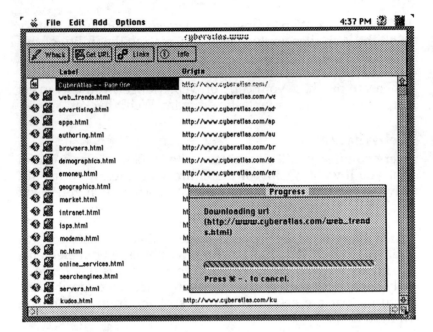

In using this product, you should be sensitive to copyright issues. You are, in fact, creating a replica of someone's creative efforts, so your use of this information should reflect sensitivity to this fact. Another caution is to be sure you have plenty of free disk space for the resulting files. If you try downloading an entire art museum, you may find yourself out of disk space in no time!

WebWhacker is great when I want to demonstrate a Web site to an audience and I don't have access to the Net at the time. It is also a lifesaver if you are caught in an Internet traffic jam and you can't get the pages downloaded as rapidly as you'd like. In this case, you can set up WebWhacker to download the site in the wee hours of the morning when the traffic is lighter. The complete site will be there for your use when you get up in the morning!

Educational Sites

Today's mantra seems to be, The Web Changes Everything. This viewpoint is being accepted by an increasing number of businesses and communities who are finding that the Web provides a new way to reach people and to provide services.

Education is not immune from the changes that are taking the rest of the world by storm. In fact, it stands to gain the most from this powerful tool — yet schools seem to be the last enterprises to take modern technology seriously.

On the surface, too many schools appear virtually unchanged from those we attended many years ago. Some pundits have even gone so far as to suggest that the technology that has had the most recent and far reaching impact on education was the school bus. Others argue that the modern copying machine deserves this honor.

Reality is not so dismal. Computers have been brought into schools, and pockets of innovation are breaking out all over the world as modern technologies are being used in effective ways. Still, we have far to go if we, as a nation, want to seriously redefine educational practice.

Let's look at California, for example. The California State Department of Education commissioned a study on technology in schools (http://goldmine.cde.ca.gov/WWW/ccc_task/ ccc.htm). Among the tidbits in this report was the finding that, while the overall student/computer ratio in California schools was 14 to one, when the study was restricted to computers capable of accessing the Web, the ratio jumped to 73:1!

Imagine how effective pencils would be if one pencil had to be shared by 73 students.

Computers, of course, are not the only technology of importance. Communication lines are missing in most of America's classrooms, causing Jim Mecklenberger to quip that schools were the last great unwired enterprise in America.

Because of massive "barn-raising" (like NetDay (http://www. netday96.com)), efforts to wire our schools this picture is improving. Similar aggressive efforts in the hardware domain can bring the computer infrastructure into the '90's for our students just in time for them to enter the workforce of the next century.

But so what?

Just because high-tech multimedia gizmos can cast their multi-hued glow on the cherubic faces of our children doesn't mean their minds are getting anything of value. An outmoded curricular and pedagogical model does not suddenly get better when it is delivered over the Web.

Does the Web have something of value to offer to our students?

The answer is yes, provided that Web-using educators understand that their role in this world will be completely different from the role they assumed in the book-based world.

Teachers and textbooks dominated instruction for the last several hundred years, and the student was largely seen as a vessel into which disjointed pieces of information were shoveled for later regurgitation on a test. The popularity of television quiz shows like Jeopardy perpetuate the perception that disjointed facts are useful in and of themselves.

Here's the problem. Any Web user has access to more information than could be taught in any school. With a few clicks of the mouse, students can go to the Library of Congress or hundreds of other incredible collections of information. New advances in science are posted on the Web weeks or months before they appear in traditional print journals. Giving even more information to these students doesn't make sense in a Web-wise world.

Imagine this scenario. A student has, at home, access to 50 channels of cable television (including Discovery Channel, Arts and Entertainment, The History Channel, PBS). In the next room there's a computer with Web access so the student can search through incredibly rich collections of literature, scientific information, etc. Add to this e-mail with other students, and education-focused on-line chat rooms, and the family den suddenly becomes mission control for learning.

Now, every weekday morning, this same student trudges off to school clutching her gaily painted lunch bucket to take her place in an unwired classroom using outdated textbooks presided over by a teacher wielding the awesome power of a sheet of slate and a stick of chalk.

Do you see a problem here?

If I were an educator who saw himself as a primary provider of information, I'd be in big trouble.

And yet, even though many educators know that the transformation of education lies right around the corner, the resistance to change in some quarters is incredibly high.

I've spent a lot of time thinking about the reasons for this resistance, and found an insight that might shed some light on the topic.

Traditional educators are right to feel threatened because the Web largely renders the previous model of education (one based on content delivery) obsolete. The last time something of this magnitude happened was in the Middle Ages when the mass-produced book was introduced to the world.

Gutenberg's Galaxy

Many credit Gutenberg for the mass-produced book, since he was the one who introduced moveable type to Europe. History shows, however, that he was perfectly content to just print books for those who already knew how to read. Universal literacy was not on his agenda.

Aldus Manutius had a different goal, however. By publishing (in 1501) the works of Virgil in Italian (and by using a small but legible typeface that we today call Italic), he created inexpensive books that could be read by those who did not read Latin. Largely through his efforts, and those of his followers (many of whom led short careers, with a flaming finish at the stake,) literacy spread throughout parts of Europe.

Schools, however, resisted using these new-fangled printed books. As Marshall McLuhan used to recount in his lectures, the teachers of the time were hired for their precise diction, and students transcribed the teacher's readings into personal copies of books they created by hand. Once the pre-printed book entered the scene, many teachers of the day (properly) felt threatened. They understood that their role was about to change forever, and nothing in their own educational background had prepared them for a change of this magnitude.

Today's teachers are feeling the same anxieties, I would guess, as those felt by their forebears from the early Renaissance. Furthermore, they are denied a once popular form of redress. While Gates, Grove, Jobs, and others of their ilk are occasionally pilloried in the educational press (read any of Neil Postman's recent writings, for example), we generally frown on burning our pioneers at the stake.

It took many years for books to be accepted in schools. One can be sure that schools that did not ultimately make the transition went out of business.

While nothing in our recent experience has prepared us for today's reality, the same kinds of changes are happening now. The genie can not be pushed back into the bottle. Our students won't let it happen. They know the truth. They know that the Web offers more information than they could explore in a thousand lifetimes, and they even know that they need guidance in how to make meaning from the incredible resources they navigate from the privacy of their bedrooms.

Most importantly they know that teachers who are not changing their practice in ways that address student needs in a wired world are fast becoming irrelevant to the educational process.

More to the point, many parents are coming to this conclusion as well.

So what are we to do?

I think we need to look at modern technology with new eyes: to see computers not as tools with which we can perform old jobs better, but as engines that power completely new tasks. Our model of education must change at its core in order for the breakthroughs of the communications revolution to take hold. We must shift from thinking of schools as sources of information to places where students learn how to make meaning from the information they find.

This is a fundamental shift in thinking about the role of educators that cuts across all subject areas. Our students will continue to be expected to gain mastery in a variety of skills and subjects. What is changing is the manner in which these skills are acquired. An educational system that meets the needs of today's learners acknowledges that knowledge is dynamic, not static; that context is more important than content; that learning is lifelong and integrated.

Schools that fail to make the transition to the new paradigm will cease to exist.

Fortunately, the Web is as powerful a resource for educators as it is for students. Education is a dominant theme of many Web pages. Any attempt to provide a thorough list of educational resources is impossible, so I won't even try. Fortunately, your favorite search engines will bring you in contact with many more resources than we could even hint at in the pages that follow.

The remainder of this chapter highlights just a few of the thousands of education-related sites available today. Most of the sites I reference are informational. In other words, they are repositories of information that (if it were practical) could conceivably be placed in books.

I will also have a bit to say about student-created Web pages, and the use of student-generated materials as assessment vehicles. The tools needed to create Web pages will be explored in a later chapter.

So, for now, let's look at some interesting educational sites!

Libraries

Libraries represent our extra-somatic memory. But books are fragile documents.

One of the ways that conquering despots can demoralize the conquered is by destroying their libraries. Whether it is the burning of the library of Alexandria in the 7th century, (http://www.perseus.tufts.edu/~ellen/AlexandrianDecline.html), or the British burning of the United States Library of Congress during the War of 1812, library destruction has long been both a symbolic and concrete way to attempt destruction of a society's long-term memory.

Now that we have the Web, historical works can be archived as non-flammable bits scattered on hard-drives all over the world. The destruction of one site would merely result in another one popping up in a few hours someplace else on the planet.

On a less philosophical level, on-line libraries bring vast amounts of information to those whose communities could not afford to house and maintain a physical collection.

Today's Web-based libraries contain a staggering amount of information, yet the size of these collections is still growing exponentially.

A few interesting collections available for free over the Web are described below.

Library of Congress

Vice President Al Gore frequently recounts his dream of a child in his hometown of Carthage, Tennessee being able to log on to the Library of Congress.

The idea of easy access to the world's libraries from towns of any size is quite compelling. The Library of Congress holds over 100 million documents — a collection that would stretch 523 miles were it all on one shelf. Access to the physical collection of this library is restricted to adults who must wait from two to four hours for documents to be manually retrieved. Electronic access to this collection is as exciting a concept for residents of Washington, D.C. as it is for those who live in places far remote from any decent library!

While the issues of copyright preclude (so far) the digital distribution of modern works, many of the more interesting documents in the Library of Congress are in the public domain. As part of a digital libraries initiative, the Library of Congress is planning to have over one million documents freely available to the public by the year 2000.

The Library of Congress Website (http://www.loc.gov) is a gateway to many services. The Thomas archive on legislative information, a list of documents in the library's collection, and a rapidly growing collection of historical documents can be accessed by anyone with a Web connection.

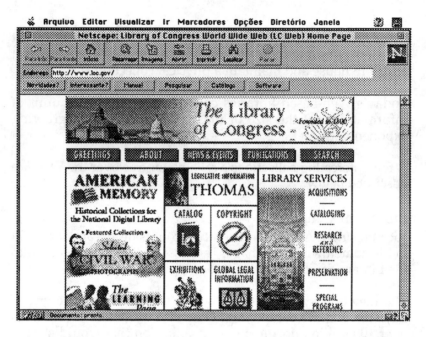

The American Memory project is digitizing thousands of historical documents, photographs, movie clips and sound files for public access through its portion of the Library of Congress site (lcweb2.loc.gov/ammem/ammemhome.html).

AMERICAN MEMORY

Historical Collections for the National Digital Library

SEARCH
American Memory Collections

BROWSE
List of all American Memory
Collections

LEARN
Organized help for using the
collections

American Memory consists of primary source and archival materials relating to American culture and history. These *digitized collections* are the key contribution of the Library of Congress to the National Digital Library. Most of these offerings are from the Library's unparalleled special collections.

Among the photo collections that have already been posted, the compelling Civil War pictures taken by Matthew Brady and his colleagues are a special treat.

Using the search engine associated with this rich database, I was able to find my Great Grandfather in three seconds! It is virtually impossible to convey the impact of seeing an ancestor reaching across space and time to appear, like magic, on the screen in front of me!

The popularity of this site has grown markedly since it was launched.

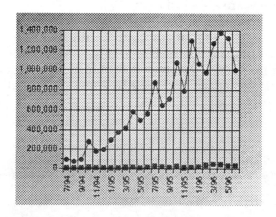

While the monthly downloads from access points outside the Library of Congress fluctuates, they now run in the range of over one million documents per month. Contrast the rapidly growing rate of access from homes, schools, and businesses (the upper curve) from the access of these documents from within the Library itself (the lower curve), and the power of digital libraries suddenly becomes crystal clear!

For young students, physical access to the Library is denied, even if you live in Washington. The Web-version of the library is open to all, every day of the year.

The Vice-President's dream is fast becoming reality as the Library of Congress enhances its Web presence.

Students are not the only beneficiaries of the Library's Web site. For educators, a special section has been created (http://lcweb2.loc.gov/ammem/ndlpedu) containing cross-disciplinary lessons and other support materials.

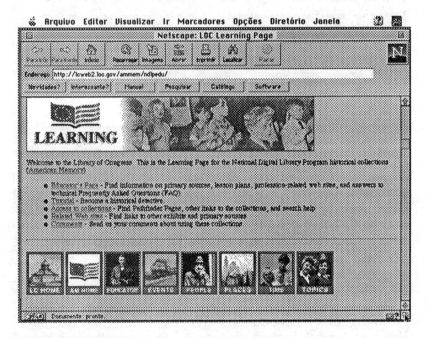

So, along with the collection itself, the library also provides tools for its effective use in education.

National Archives

The National Archives contain incredible resources, some of which are being made available on the Web (http://www.nara.gov).

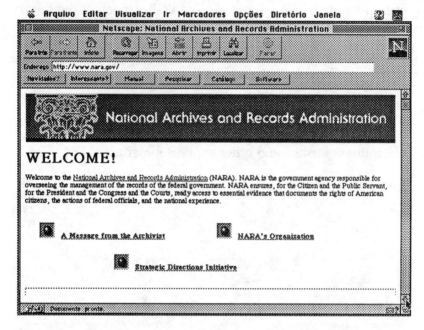

In addition to housing the originals of the Declaration of Independence, the Constitution, Bill of Rights, and other great documents of U.S. history, the archives also have a copy of the Magna Carta on display. All of these documents, along with background materials, are available for downloading by on-line visitors.

As with the Library of Congress, the National Archives has classroom materials available as well (http://www.nara.gov/nara/digital/classroom.htm). While the collection was small the last time I looked, I expect the educational support materials will be expanded in the future.

On-line Books

Photographs and short historical documents are not the only items to be found in on-line libraries. Complete transcriptions of literary works are available as well.

The collections are eclectic, to be sure, and are driven by the expiration of copyrights, and the interest of those who have the heroic task of typing (or scanning) in classical works of literature.

Carnegie-Mellon University maintains a searchable index of thousands of complete books that are available for free from a variety of on-line repositories (http://www.cs.cmu.edu/Web/books.html).

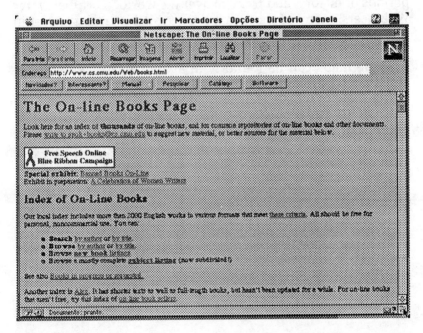

While today's computers are poor substitutes for the portability and legibility of paper books, digital versions of books have their own utility. First, readers with vision impairments can display on-line books at any type size they wish, or can even have the book read to them out loud. Second, researchers looking for the context of a quotation can use their word processor to quickly locate a passage to be examined.

Rather than replacing printed books, I see on-line manuscripts as yet another companion for avid readers.

PCL Map Collection

Perhaps your interest lies in the area of maps — historical, or modern. In this case, the PCL map collection at the University of Texas deserves your attention (http://www.lib.utexas.edu/Libs/PCL/Map_collection/Map_collection.htm). The physical collection consists of about 250,000 maps from many periods of history, and from all over the world. Fortunately for Web users, many of these maps are available from the Net in high-resolution color images.

Antique maps can be found with as much ease as the latest aerial photograph maps from the U.S. Geological Survey, such as this view of the area surrounding San Francisco's Telegraph Hill. (Our San Francisco office is in the light "C-shaped" building at the top of the picture.)

Encyclopedias

While you can locate many encyclopedia sites on the Web, I am choosing to highlight only one.

For two hundred years, Encyclopaedia Britannica (EB) ruled the encyclopedia world. They were first because they were best. But even the mighty can fall, and this is exactly what happened to this giant a few years ago when they dropped from number one to the number three spot in the reference market. Worst of all (to the traditionalists), EB's fall from grace was driven not by other encyclopedia publishers, but by two CD-ROM's! It is as if the works of Shakespeare were eclipsed by comic books.

In staging a just-in-time recovery, Encyclopaedia Britannica made an ingenious move to the Web (http://www.eb.com) where they quickly reasserted their status as the number-one supplier of reference information in the world.

Each year, many thousands of college students find they have on-line access to this dynamic reference work because their college or university has established a subscription for all the students. Annual personal subscriptions are $150/year — a cheap price to pay for access to a work of this magnitude.

The encyclopedia is easy enough to use. Just enter a request in plain English and, more likely than not, you'll be taken directly to the reference information you are seeking. For example, the request "What was Farnsworth's role in the invention of television?" produced this result:

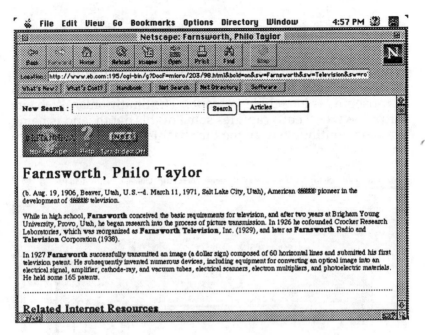

Farnsworth, Philo Taylor

(b. Aug. 19, 1906, Beaver, Utah, U.S.--d. March 11, 1971, Salt Lake City, Utah), American ▓▓▓▓ pioneer in the development of ▓▓▓▓ television.

While in high school, **Farnsworth** conceived the basic requirements for television, and after two years at Brigham Young University, Provo, Utah, he began research into the process of picture transmission. In 1926 he cofounded Crocker Research Laboratories, which was reorganized as **Farnsworth Television**, Inc. (1929), and later as **Farnsworth** Radio and **Television** Corporation (1938).

In 1927 **Farnsworth** successfully transmitted an image (a dollar sign) composed of 60 horizontal lines and submitted his first television patent. He subsequently invented numerous devices, including equipment for converting an optical image into an electrical signal, amplifier, cathode-ray, and vacuum tubes, electrical scanners, electron multipliers, and photoelectric materials. He held some 165 patents.

Related Internet Resources

What makes this Web-based encyclopedia so useful is that it is updated continuously — an impossible task in the world of print. For anyone interested in getting reliable high-quality background information on virtually any topic, the Web-based Encyclopaedia Britannica is a bargain.

109

Museums

The Smithsonian

Whenever I work in Washington, DC, I try to schedule an extra
day to visit one of the Smithsonian museums. This collection
of museums is incredible in scope. The Smithsonian Web site
(http://www.si.edu) captures some of this depth, and is being
updated continuously as the Smithsonian celebrates its 150th
anniversary in 1996.

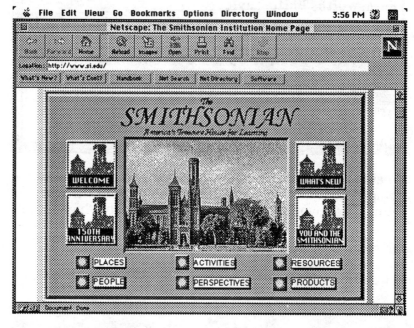

Visitors are provided with a map of the Mall along which
many of the Smithsonian museums are located. By clicking on
a photograph of a building, the visitor is brought inside where
some of the exhibitions are on display for Web visitors.

As with many other museum sites, the Smithsonian provides
an educators' page (http://educate.si.edu/intro.html)
complete with lesson plans connected to various on-line
exhibits.

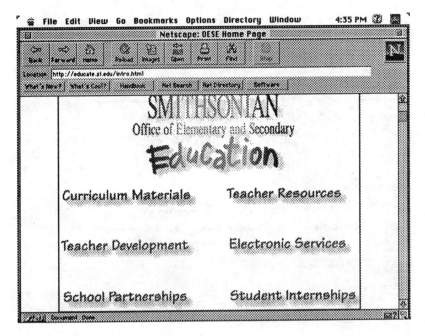

Netscape: OESE Home Page

http://educate.si.edu/intro.html

SMITHSONIAN
Office of Elementary and Secondary
Education

Curriculum Materials   Teacher Resources

Teacher Development   Electronic Services

School Partnerships   Student Internships

While the on-line collections are far from complete, they provide a tremendous educational resource to anyone who visits.

Franklin Institute Science Museum

The Franklin Institute Science Museum is the granddad of hands-on museums. As a young child, I visited Philadelphia with my parents and they took me to this wonderful place. It was the first museum I'd seen where you did more than look at static exhibits!

Their on-line museum (http://sln.fi.edu/tfi/welcome.html) brings much of their interactive philosophy to educators all over the world through a series of lesson plans on a wide range of topics.

For example, an in-depth lesson plan on wind provides a series of experiments, each allowing students to explore a different aspect of moving air.

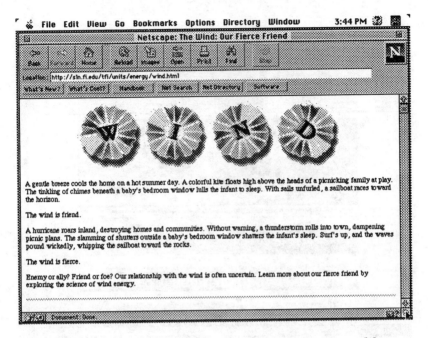

A gentle breeze cools the home on a hot summer day. A colorful kite floats high above the heads of a picnicking family at play. The tinkling of chimes beneath a baby's bedroom window lulls the infant to sleep. With sails unfurled, a sailboat races toward the horizon.

The wind is friend.

A hurricane roars inland, destroying homes and communities. Without warning, a thunderstorm rolls into town, dampening picnic plans. The slamming of shutters outside a baby's bedroom window shatters the infant's sleep. Surf's up, and the waves pound wickedly, whipping the sailboat toward the rocks.

The wind is fierce.

Enemy or ally? Friend or foe? Our relationship with the wind is often uncertain. Learn more about our fierce friend by exploring the science of wind energy.

Document: Done

This site is a great resource for educators and learners alike.

The Exploratorium

If the Franklin Museum is one of the oldest hands-on museums, the Exploratorium is one of the most exciting. This incredible museum is reallyt a science playground located in San Francisco's Palace of Fine Arts. Tour buses and school groups alike crowd the halls every day and the air is filled with the joyous noise of young and old alike making science real through experiments they conduct themselves. To the first-time visitor, the Exploratorium looks chaotic, but it quickly becomes apparent that activities are grouped around various sense-based phenomena relating to optics, sound, kinesthetics, etc.

The Exploratorium Web site (http://www.exploratorium.edu) replicates much of the experience of visiting the actual museum. Instead of providing static exhibits with printed information, the site takes full advantage of media — sounds, Shockwave files, etc., to bring the Exploratorium to life.

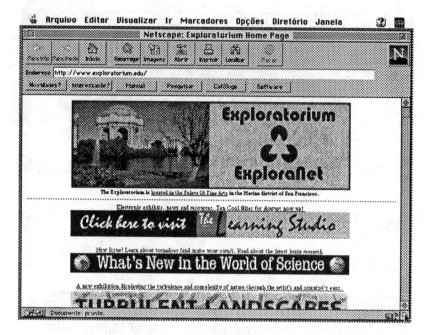

If you are anywhere near San Francisco, you should visit the Exploratorium itself. In the meantime, their site will provide hours of insightful exploration for participants of any age.

The Web Museum

My college art appreciation class used a textbook by Janson that is still being used thirty years later! This textbook (with mostly black and white images) was supplemented by lectures in which my professor showed a tray or two of yellowing 35mm slides illustrating the works he considered to be important.

By allocating twelve weeks to the period from pre-history to the Renaissance, there was lots of art, but little appreciation. A course that should have been a delight became drudgery instead. Fortunately, I lived in Chicago at the time and could visit one of the world's great museums (Chicago's Art Institute) whenever I wanted to see what art really looked like. Since then, I've been blessed with opportunities to visit great art museums all over the world.

For most students, this access is not possible — at least not when they are in school. Fortunately, a grant from the BMW Foundation has made the Web Museum possible. This incredible Web site (http://www.emf.net/louvre) contains a deep and broad collection of paintings from all periods of history, and from museums all over the world.

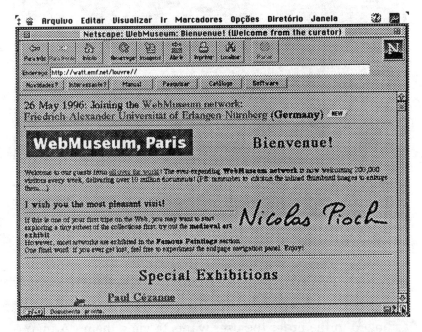

Visitors can browse through a list of artists' names, for example, and then get in-depth information about the artist and his or her artwork. Representative samples of the artist's work are on display in the form of high-resolution JPEG images in which the scans were done with care and precision to preserve the nuance of color and tone. These images can be downloaded for free use by educators. Some of the works even have essays connected with them!

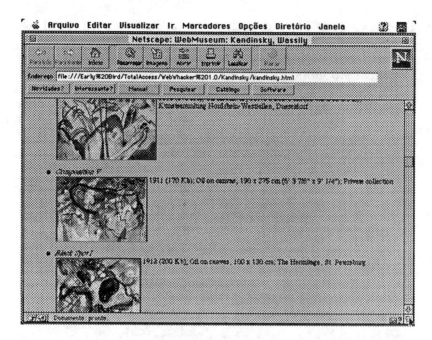

A modern-day art appreciation class could make extensive use of this site by having students explore particular artists or periods on their own, and then assemble their own slide show to share with their classmates.

For Macintosh users, the free programs called Show and JPEGView (both available from http://www.shareware.com) make digital slide show creation a snap. Show provides a "slide tray" on which small thumbnails of each image can be arranged in the order the user wants to view them. A menu-based slide show command then launches JPEGView to bring the full-screen color slide show to the monitor. For a classroom equipped with a high-resolution color projection system, the results exceed those of the faded 35mm slides you might remember from your college days! Because JPEGView automatically creates optimized palettes for each image, the colors are bright and crisp.

The only problem with the Web Museum is that you lose all sense of time while exploring this incredibly rich site. It is a true feast for the eyes!

Index of on-line museums

If you are interested in visiting other museums and zoos on-line, this site (http://www.comlab.ox.ac.uk/archive/other/museums.html) provides an excellent gateway to collections all over the world.

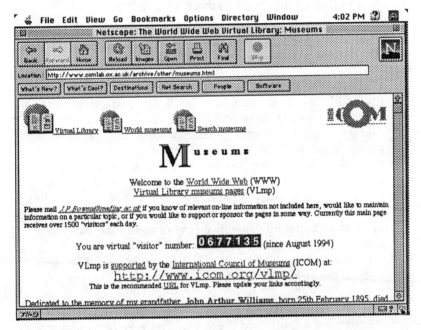

Museums are listed by country, and many of them can be explored either in English or in the dominant language of the country in which they are located. Not all of the museum listings include exhibits. Some just describe the museum, list its hours of operation, and describe the highlights of its collections. Others are quite rich sites filled with in-depth explorations of their content.

This list is a tremendous resource for anyone looking for on-line museums to explore.

Zoos

Our fascination with animals is amazing. Years ago, I consulted for a marine animal park. Every day I would see thousands of people clamoring to see all the fascinating animals on display. While I saw the advantages of people being able to see these amazing creatures, I felt sad that these animals had been deprived of their natural habitat.

Years later, in 1994, I wrote the following piece of fiction that was published in *Electronic Learning* magazine:

While it was among the last to repatriate its collection to the wild, the San Francisco Zoo's conversion to total virtuality went quite smoothly. The zoos of the twentieth century, with their caged collections of animals deprived of their range and natural environment, were outlawed through a rider to the International Biodiversity Treaty of 2006. Many zoos had already made the move toward virtual collections long before, since electronic access to multimedia exhibits of animals in their natural habitats provided a better informational environment than most zoos could provide with live animals. Pioneering work in multimedia exhibits by the Indianapolis and National Zoos in the 1990's set the stage for the transition to come.

The conversions started poorly as many of the animals had a hard time adapting to the wild. "Halfway houses" were established around the world to assist in animal repatriation, and by the second decade of the century, strategies had been developed to help nearly all animals readapt to their natural surroundings.

The zoologists remained, of course, even as the San Francisco Zoo became a presence on the Net: http://www.SFZoo.edu. Scholarship involved more field work. The presence of zoos on the Net meant that visitors could examine any virtual zoo with equal ease. Competition for visitors was based on the variety and accuracy of each collection.

***

Claudia stood among her classmates, her palms sweating, as she described the proposal for her senior project. She explained that her love of animals drew her to suggest a field trip into the jungles of Costa Rica. The last accurate count of the endangered mono tití squirrel monkey had been made thirty years before, in the 1990's. The virtual exhibit at www.SFZoo.edu was outdated, and she wanted to gather the data to bring it up to date.

Her classmates asked a few questions about the project, volunteered some ideas, and, along with her mentors, gave overwhelming support to her project.

The memory of this support was jarred loose as the shuttle craft from San José set down on the gravel landing strip in Quepos. While most parts of Costa Rica were served by more comfortable transportation devices, this area had locked into the past to preserve its pristine beauty. The Electrobus ride into town, past the area's only remaining banana plantation, gave Claudia a chance to check out her field gear. Her Newton's color screen flashed on as the internal system software went through its checkout. The global positioning subsystem worked perfectly. Every note she took, every image or sound she recorded, would be stamped with the date, time, relative humidity, temperature, and latitude and longitude measured to an accuracy of one meter. More accurate instruments were available, of course, but her budget of $150 limited her to this modest device.

The completion of the Global Information Infrastructure along the Pacific coast of Central America insured that her digital cellular link would keep her in contact with her classmates, teachers, and zoologists all over the world. As she checked her fanny pack, she was relieved to find several gigabyte memory cards — enough to provide local backup for her data gathering in the unlikely event that the Net went down during the rains.

The next morning, Claudia started exploring the Manuel Antonio National Park. By the time she waded across the river to the park's entrance, her boots were caked with mud. How different this was from jacking into the virtual zoos! No one got muddy moving a mouse, she thought.

She climbed up a coastal hill, past iguanas and coatimundis oblivious to her presence, until she was level with the canopy of mangroves and other dense trees so essential to the habitat of the mono tití. As the sun came up, the morning concert began. Birds of all kinds filled the air with their distinctive calls. Claudia captured a few bird calls on her Newton. Ever since the discovery that bird calls were recursive fractals, bird recognition software had become much more accurate. She had downloaded the database for the 850 birds common to Costa Rica, and smiled with satisfaction as the names and color pictures of the birds she was hearing appeared on her screen.

In a few moments, the jungle became quieter, and then she heard it — a sound somewhat like a bird call, but clearly generated by another animal. In the distance she could see tree branches bouncing up and down as something was moving from tree to tree across the canopy. Within a minute, the sounds became much louder and she could see the black tufted tails of her red-furred quarry. The area was soon filled with chattering squirrel monkeys — hundreds of them. Immediately she started recording the sounds and images of these lovely creatures. How beautiful they looked! Their faces were so delicate — much like a human baby's!

As she captured pictures of individual animals, she launched the pattern recognition scanner, dropped in one of her close-up monkey images, and left it running in the background to provide an accurate monkey count. She could scarcely believe what she saw. In the 1990's there were only ten troops of mono titís left, with about 70 monkeys in each troop. Yet, in front of her were over 200 active animals in one troop working their way northward through the trees!

Later in the day, she talked with long-time residents of the area who explained that, many years ago, land development and roads had severely restricted the habitat of this animal. Because these animals need treetops to jump between, the creation of a single road could isolate a troop. If the isolated area was too small, the troop would die out. Once this was understood, "monkey bridges" were planted everywhere in the area, expanding the range of these animals immensely, saving them from certain extinction, and increasing the jungle for all to enjoy.

***

The day before she went home, Claudia sat in a seafood restaurant in the sleepy coastal town of Quepos. As a steady tropical rain splattered the restaurant's tin roof, she uploaded her data to the San Francisco Zoo Website and started working on her report for school. A green parrot perched near her table, waiting for the rain to clear. Suddenly, she became aware of an old Gringo looking at her from across the room. His shoulder-length hair and long beard were silver gray. His weathered face held eyes still full of life. Spindly legs emerged from his shorts, and he sported a faded T-shirt she could almost read — something about Woodstock '94, whatever that was.

"Hi," the stranger said as he came by her table. He was enchanted by the equipment she was using. "My name's Steve. What's yours?"

"Claudia," she said with hesitation.

"That's a nice rig you've got, can I see it?"

121

"Sure," said Claudia as she demonstrated it to the stranger. As she explained her project, a smile expanded across Steve's face and the tanned wrinkles around his eyes almost obscured his vision.

"This is what I always dreamed about," he sighed. "Placing power in the hands of kids, using computers as tools for thinking — truly liberating the minds of all learners to achieve anything they can dream!"

He grasped her arm. "Tell me, have you ever heard the phrase 'bicycle for the mind?' I used it once, many years ago, to describe the idea that humans are pretty slow, compared with other mammals. Yet, once they invented the bicycle, humans could outpace any animal on the planet. I saw computers acting as magnifiers for thinking for students everywhere..."

"What's a bicycle?" Claudia interrupted, pulling her arm away.

"Never mind, you're too young. Just like I was once."

Steve's gaze shifted into the distance as he thought back to his childhood in Cupertino, California and his dream of personal computing. How could he expect today's youngsters to appreciate what it was like to have lived in those days — an era where computers were bound to a desktop by the twin cords of power and telecommunications lines. Now everything was wireless. Solar charged fuel cells extended battery life indefinitely, and produced pure water as a waste product. Technology was transparent. All Claudia had to do was concentrate on her research project. She probably never knowingly formatted a disk in her life.

No, Steve thought, she wouldn't understand.

The sky cleared and Steve walked along the waterfront, pausing just long enough to watch a small lizard emerge to sun itself. He smiled again, realizing that his dreams had

122

all come true, and suddenly he felt very old. Very old indeed.

Since this piece was written, much of what I described has become technically possible. Will zoos change in the future? Some are using the Web to expand their role today.

National Zoological Park
The National Zoological Park (http://www.si.edu/organiza/museums/zoo/homepage/nzphome.htm) is part of the Smithsonian Institution. Its Web site provides a rich array of information on many of the animals in its collection, complete with excellent photographs.

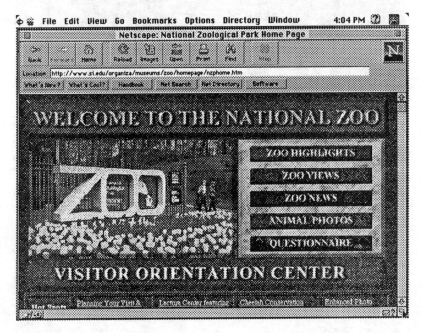

Users wanting information on a particular animal can browse through the zoo's collection and study the habitat, diet, and behaviors of animals from all over the world.

While virtual zoos lack the face-to-face quality of seeing animals in a park, remember that in most cases the zoological park habitats are quite removed from those the animals occupy in their natural surroundings. Resources such as Web-based zoos might, someday, provide links to observation centers in the wild.

Index of zoo sites

If you are looking for the Web-version of a particular zoo, you'll want to explore http://www.mindspring.com/~zoonet/www_virtual_lib/zoos.html. This incredible listing provides gateways to Web sites for zoos located all over the world.

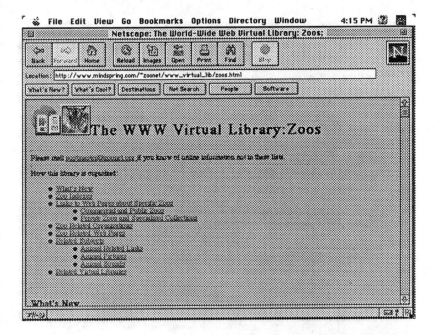

Many of these sites just contain information on the zoo, its operating hours, and fees. Other sites contain a rich array of information ranging from details on the animals in their collections to lesson plans for educators to use with their students.

For example, the Indianapolis Zoo (http://www.indyzoo.com) provides photos of some of its many animals taken at different times of the year.

The pictures at this site are placed in the public domain so students can incorporate them in their reports.

The zoo's site also provides a "homework helper" where students can get more detailed information on animals they may be studying.

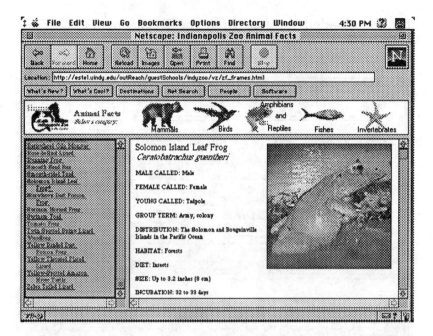

As with many of the museum sites on the Web, education's connections to the zoological parks are facilitated through this highly interactive medium.

Governmental educational resources

Many valuable resources for students and teachers alike are funded with government money. By placing these resources on the Web, any student, educator or parent interested in them can get copies for free. Resources are found on Web sites associated with federal, state, and school district offices. While I will mention only a few, you will surely want to explore the broad range of other governmental education resource sites available to you.

The United States Department of Education

The United States Department of Education generates many valuable documents each year focusing on different aspects of education. These documents and other support materials can be downloaded for free from the Department's Web site (http://www.ed.gov).

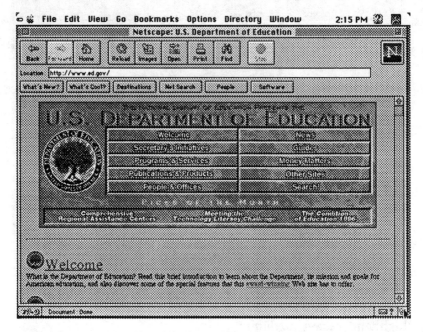

Current topics of interest to many educators involve the effective use of technology in education, and ways to bridge the gap between school and work. This site has enough valuable resources to warrant frequent visits — especially if you are involved in efforts to restructure education in your community.

AskERIC
ERIC (The Educational Resources Information Center) (http://ericir.syr.edu) is a tremendously valuable information network for educators, supported by Syracuse University with strong connections to the U.S. Department of Education and other agencies.

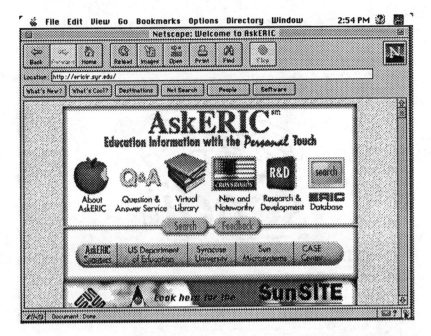

In addition to a searchable database of educational materials, the AskERIC feature allows librarians, educators, students, parents and others to ask questions about educational resources and to receive personalized responses at no cost! While this site is not glamorous, it is tremendously useful, and you'll find yourself heading there frequently to get information on just about any aspect of education.

SENDIT

Most states have their own Web site devoted to education. North Dakota's site, http://www.sendit.nodak.edu, is particularly well done.

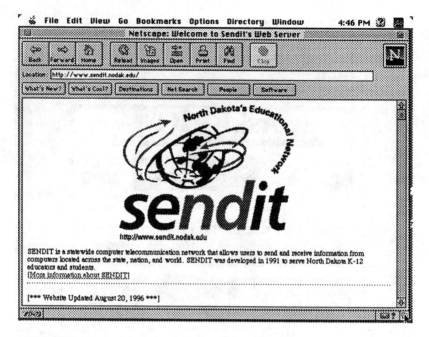

North Dakota's Educational Network

sendit

http://www.sendit.nodak.edu

SENDIT is a statewide computer telecommunication network that allows users to send and receive information from computers located across the state, nation, and world. SENDIT was developed in 1991 to serve North Dakota K-12 educators and students.
[More information about SENDIT]

[*** Website Updated August 20, 1996 ***]

SENDIT is North Dakota's statewide computer telecommunications network designed to connect educators and students in that state to the world. One of SENDIT's greatest resources is Gleason Sackman. He is one of the most active advocates for the effective use of educational telecomputing in the world. One of his resources you will find most useful is his list of school, district, and state education sites (http://www.sendit.nodak.edu/k12). This list provides links to thousands of school and government sites in every state. Furthermore, it is updated frequently. This is just one of the many valuable resources to be found at the SENDIT site.

Commercial educational sites

The education of our children is of great commercial interest. Americans spend over $200 billion on education every year, and quite a few corporations would love to have a piece of that action. The commercial participants have much to offer educators, parents and students, and quite a few of these resources are available at no direct cost to the user.

The following few sites show a piece of the educational spectrum as viewed through the prism of commercial vendors.

Discovery Channel School

Many educators, parents and students enjoy the television programming offered by the Discovery Channel (http://www.discovery.com). In addition to educational television, the Discovery Channel School Web site (http://school.discovery.com) provides a rich resource for additional materials and activities.

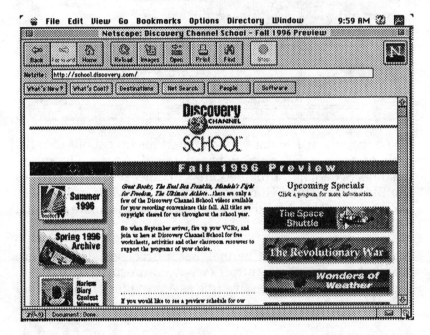

For example, in August, 1996, the "Dead Inventor's Corner" had a feature article on Garrett Morgan, inventor of the gas mask and the traffic stop light.

The engaging article not only explored his inventions, but his lack of formal recognition based on his race. Discovery Channel School also provided links to other resources, such as the Black Inventor's Home Page (http://www.users.fast.net/~blc/xlhome7.htm) for those wishing to conduct more research on the topic.

Now that Discovery Channel has purchased The Nature Company retail chain (http://www.natureco.com), it could easily take a more aggressive role as a provider of educational content.

Computer Curriculum Corporation

Computer Curriculum Corporation (CCC) is a major provider of integrated learning systems to schools. In addition to their line of software designed to help students with basic skills, they have created a Web site (http://www.cccnet.com) containing structured lessons.

Teachers and parents can become members of CCCNet and gain access to lesson materials for use in the classroom or home.

The material on CCCNet is more structured than that in the Discovery Channel School, in keeping with the approach found in most of CCC's materials. I mention this site, primarily, because it is possible that CCC will announce its intentions to offer a complete school curriculum through the Web.

Family Education Network

The Family Education Network (http://www.families.com) provides a wide array of support information for families who want to take an active involvement in their children's education.

Through the use of thematically grouped links to Web sites, families using this tool as a launching pad can find materials appropriate for learners of any age from early elementary through high school.

The goal of this site is to provide resources for everyone who wants to ensure that their children have a high-quality education.

On-line schools and universities

With all the tremendous educational resources available on the Web, you might ask, "Why not just put the schools there?" In fact, this is starting to happen, especially in higher education.

When the University of California eliminated its affirmative action program, I think it missed a golden opportunity to announce that *every* applicant would be admitted to UC-on-line for their freshman and sophomore years. Students who completed these programs could then apply for entry to a physical campus for their last two years, if they wished.

By having an on-line option, the UC system could have avoided dealing with the limitations of a bricks and mortar university, and could have extended its reach to the many thousands of tuition-bearing students looking for a place to get their degrees.

Instead, the Powers That Be decided that exclusivity was more important than addressing the common good, and it will be curious to see what happens to the system over the next few years.

High-quality college programs are now available to students world-wide through a mixture of traditional correspondence courses and the Web. As the following sites show, this field is moving quickly!

Open University of the United Kingdom

Imagine a university with over 200,000 students and no campus! The Open University is the largest school in the UK. Over 25% of UK's college students attend this institution from their home towns. Courses use a combination of video (broadcast on BBC), books, small group meetings, and the Internet.

The Open University Web site (http://www.open.ac.uk) provides background information on this school along with links to some of the course materials.

While the Web will play an increasingly important role in the future, only a few courses are offered through the Web at this time.

The Open University already provides courses for students in other countries, and its increased use of the Web makes it one of the premiere providers of post-secondary education worldwide. As the first university designed for distance learning, the Open University has a head start in providing a quality education for students who don't have the time or resources to attend school on a traditional campus.

Colleges and universities world-wide will find on-line schools to be fearsome competitors.

ME/U On-line

Mind Extension University (ME/U) was developed by Glenn Jones (of Jones Intercable) as a U.S. variant of the Open University. The ME/U cable channel provides a lot of interesting instructional programming, and its Web site (http://www.meu.edu) provides additional resources.

Learners interested in a formal education can sign up for degree programs at any of several colleges and universities associated with ME/U, including the University of Colorado, George Washington University, and California State University.

Informal courses are provided primarily through the ME/U cable channel, and additional educational materials (books, videos, software) can be purchased from ME/U on-line.

Cyber High School

Colleges and universities are not the only ones exploring the power of distance learning. The Cyber High School (http://www.webcom.com/~cyberhi/welcome.html) is a private college-preparatory high school that delivers its curriculum over the Internet.

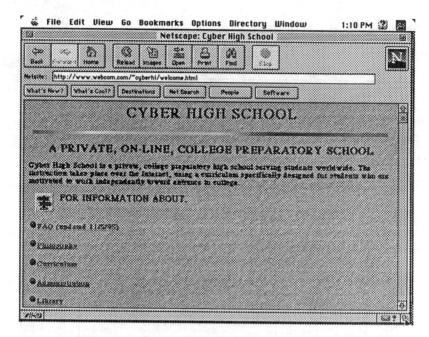

Netscape: Cyber High School

Back   Forward   Home   Reload   Images   Open   Print   Find   Stop

Netsite: http://www.webcom.com/~cyberhi/welcome.html

What's New?   What's Cool?   Destinations   Net Search   People   Software

CYBER HIGH SCHOOL

A PRIVATE, ON-LINE, COLLEGE PREPARATORY SCHOOL.

Cyber High School is a private, college preparatory high school serving students worldwide. The instruction takes place over the Internet, using a curriculum specifically designed for students who are motivated to work independently toward entrance to college.

FOR INFORMATION ABOUT:

- FAQ (updated 11/5/95)
- Philosophy
- Curriculum
- Administration
- Library

This school is designed for the highly motivated self-directed learner. Because it is Web-based, students can "attend" from virtually anywhere in the world.

Prospective students have to pass an entrance examination, and the tuition is not cheap — $4,200 per year for the 1995-1996 school year. But this is peanuts compared with that charged by traditional residential college-prep schools.

Students get plenty of one-on-one time with their instructors, and take part in peer conferences with other students world-wide. The curriculum is based on a classical model emphasizing the great works of literature, the study of history through the examination of historical documents themselves, and the use of a discovery-based approach for math and science. The one foreign language offered is Latin.

Cyber High is not "home schooling." Students interact with their teachers every day. There is a lot of flexibility in the curriculum, however, making this a particularly intriguing alternative to the traditional high school programs offered in most communities.

Fraser Valley Distance Education School
The Fraser Valley Distance Education School (http://www.fvrcs.gov.bc.ca) is one of nine public distance education schools located through out the Province of British Columbia, operating under the Ministry of Education.

It provides a complete curriculum, resources and support for students (K-12) and parents choosing a home-based educational program within the Fraser Valley region of British Columbia.

Most of their courses follow the typical correspondence format — paper based, mail delivered. However, on-line programs are planned. Some of the Grade 11 and 12 level courses are now available via the Internet.

The Fraser Valley Distance Education School provides a complete elementary program for those students not enrolled in regular school, a secondary program leading to graduation for students not enrolled in a secondary school, individual courses for students in secondary school (registered or not), and individual secondary school courses for adults who wish to complete, upgrade or enhance their education.

A complete syllabus for each course is posted on-line, and students can order the support materials directly from the school.

If you are interested in exploring other on-line schools, you should visit Yahoo's directory on distance learning (http://www.yahoo.com/Education/Alternative/Distance_Learning).

Math and Science sites

As you've seen, the Web contains incredible educational resources on many topics. The following is a very short list of valuable sites devoted to education in the areas of mathematics and science.

Your favorite search engine will locate many hundreds of great sites on these topics, but these few were chosen to illustrate some of the power that is available to any learner or educator with access to the Net.

The Ada Project

The role of women in science and technology is often left out of mainstream instruction. The Ada Project site (http://www.cs.yale.edu/homes/tap/tap.htm) fixes this problem.

The site is named after Ada Byron (Lady Lovelace) the woman who created the programs for Charles Babbage's Difference Engine (a mechanical programmable computer that used punched cards).

This site is a valuable resource on the history of women in science and technology. It provides career guidance, and listings of job openings, and provides access to articles and research studies on gender and the Web. While the site was designed by and for women, men will find it filled with valuable information as well. Any educator interested in resources to encourage women to enter the fields of science, mathematics, or technology should visit this site.

NASA

All things relating to space exploration can be found at the National Aeronautics and Space Administration's (NASA's) site (http://www.nasa.gov).

141

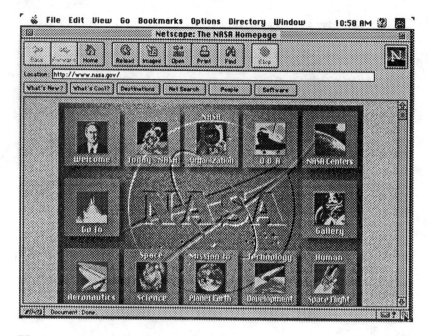

Photo archives from numerous missions, both manned and unmanned, are here for the grabbing. The latest images from the Hubble Space Telescope are here, along with an extensive collection of instructional materials.

The collection is updated frequently, so return visitors are guaranteed a treat each time they go there!

AIMS

The Activities Integrating Math and Science (AIMS) Web site (http://204.161.33.100) is a great resource for educators and students alike.

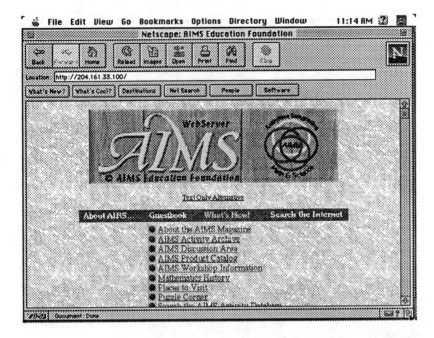

Among the many jewels posted on this site are a great collection of hands-on math activities, lesson plans, and resources on the history of mathematics and mathematicians. This site goes far beyond the traditional topics explored in the classrooms of our youth and brings powerful learning tools within the grasp of everyone who wants to learn a bit more about mathematics and its connection to science.

Eisenhower National Clearinghouse for Mathematics and Science Education

The Eisenhower National Clearinghouse for Mathematics and Science Education (ENC) is funded through a contract with the U. S. Department of Education to provide K-12 teachers with a central source of information on mathematics and science curriculum materials. Their Web site (http://www.enc.org) provides a wide variety of materials of value to educators at all grade levels.

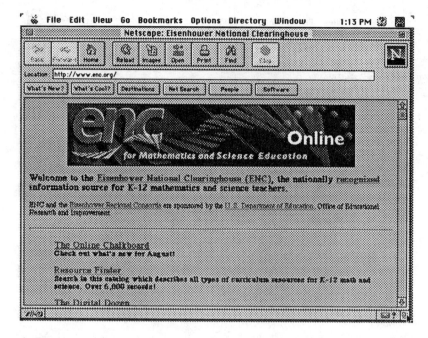

A Resource Finder includes references to print, other media (*e.g.*, video, audio, graphic images, and software), kits, and on-line electronic resources.

The ENC Web site references lots of engaging resources related to different aspects of mathematics and science, and is perfectly geared to the needs of curious students and educators alike.

The Globe Program

Vice President Gore brought two of his passions — global telecommunications and the environment — together when he suggested the creation of the Global Learning and Observations to Benefit the Environment Program (GLOBE) (http://www.globe.gov).

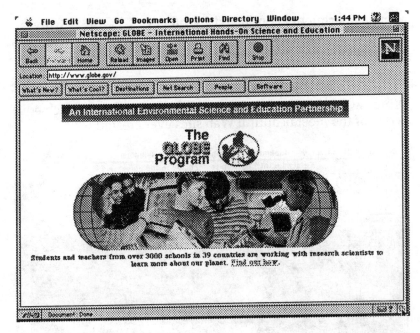

An International Environmental Science and Education Partnership

The
GLOBE
Program

Students and teachers from over 3000 schools in 39 countries are working with research scientists to learn more about our planet. Find out how.

GLOBE is a worldwide network of students, teachers, and scientists working together to study and understand the global environment.

Students make a core set of environmental observations at or near their schools and report their data via the Internet. Scientists use this data in their research and provide feedback to the students to enrich their science education. Each day, images created from the student data sets are posted on the Web, allowing students and visitors to the GLOBE site to visualize the student environmental observations.

Participants are scattered throughout the world. While the U.S. participation was started with government funds, this will be ending soon, leaving it to the private sector to keep the project alive. Some of the partnerships connected with this project are listed at the site.

To me, the beauty of this project is that it has the students doing the data gathering rather than having them just read about experiments conducted by others. GLOBE is truly an example of what can happen when students and scientists work side by side worldwide!

Windows to the Universe

Windows to the Universe (http://www.windows.umich.edu) is one of the most beautiful Web sites ever created.

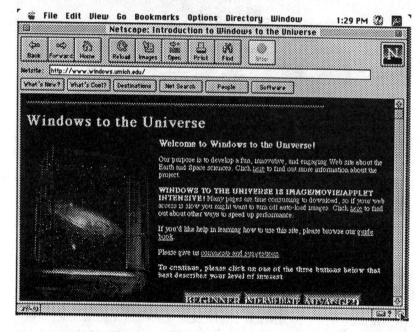

The objective of this project, funded by NASA, is to develop an innovative and engaging Web-site that spans the Earth and Space sciences using a rich array of documents that explore science along with the historical and cultural ties between science, exploration, and the human experience.

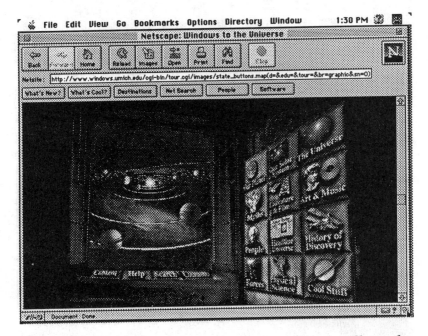

This site opened in March, 1996, and is still under construction. The approach of the site is informational rather than interactive, but the depth and scope of information will be so great, and the linkages so natural, that this site should instantly find a place in classrooms at all grade levels.

If I were a textbook publisher, this one site would have me looking for another line of work.

Other educational sites

Global School Net

It is impossible to know anything useful about this history of educational telecommunications without coming across the name of Al Rogers. This former educator brought e-mail to students worldwide and went on to create the Global School Net (GSN) Foundation (http://www.gsn.org).

This Web site contains a treasure trove of information for educators as well as a series of links to many other projects in which Al is involved. For example, the CalWeb project has students throughout California creating their own history resource materials based on research they are conducting in their own communities.

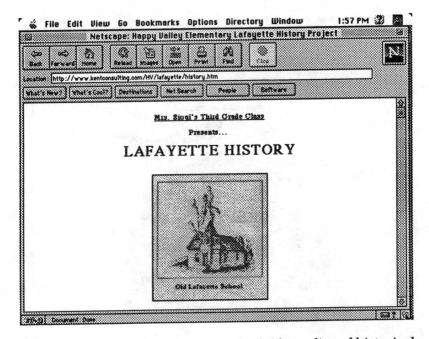

Mrs. Sioni's Third Grade Class

Presents...

LAFAYETTE HISTORY

Old Lafayette School

It is a humbling experience to see the high quality of historical resources that are collected and then shared with the world, especially when these resources are created, in some cases, by students in third grade!

New Horizons

Dee Dickenson is among the most gifted people I know. She has devoted a tremendous amount of time and effort into exploring modern pedagogical models that address the learning styles of all students. Her work builds bridges between the theory of Multiple Intelligences (developed by Harvard's Professor Howard Gardner) and the Superlearning strategies originated in Bulgaria by Professor Lazanov and his colleagues.

Her New Horizons Web site (http://www.newhorizons.org) contains a wonderful collection of resources for educators and learners alike.

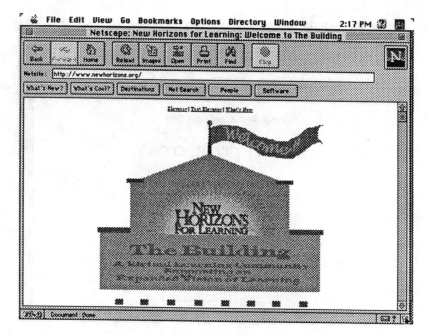

In addition to exploring education as it takes place in schools, Dee is also concerned with staff development in industry. The New Horizons site is a great launching pad for pedagogical and curricular information, worldwide.

Web 66

One of the great educational resource links in the country is the Web 66 site maintained by the University of Minnesota (http://web66.coled.umn.edu).

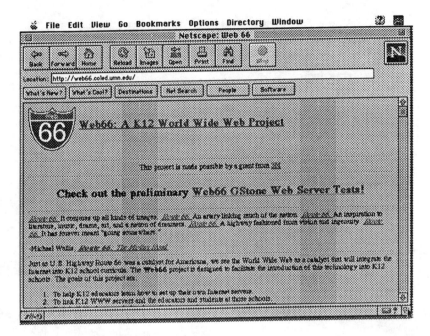

Topics covered on this site include instruction on how to set up your own educational Web pages, along with links to school sites all over the country.

Lesson plans in many subject areas are also provided here, making this site a location you'll visit again and again.

CSEARCH

Cisco, a manufacturer of Internet switching and routing hardware, sponsors a search engine with links to specific curricular areas (http://sunsite.unc.edu/cisco).

This site provides lots of support for teachers, including lesson plans in many subject areas. For example, a link to http://www.xs4all.nl/~swanson/history takes you to a very rich set of resources for teaching history with the Net. Tools like CSEARCH help educators find quality materials among the millions of documents posted on the Web.

Electronic Frontier Foundation

At first glance you might wonder why an organization promoting on-line civil rights would be listed in a chapter on education.

The Electronic Frontier Foundation (http://www.eff.org) is devoted to promoting the free interchange of information worldwide.

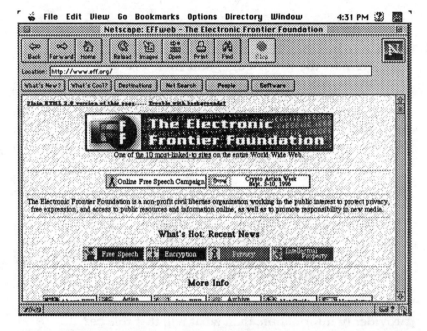

Its members are highly articulate supporters of the idea that the Bill of Rights did not expire when the Web came into existence. While their stance on some issues is bound to be controversial in some quarters (as is that of the American Civil Liberties Union), if you are concerned at all with the protection of your on-line privacy and your ability to access public information, you'll find this organization's site worth exploring.

A search on the topic of education brings up a series of speeches in defense of the power of the Web to support student learning. Many of these articles can form the basis for quite stimulating conversations with your colleagues!

Some observations...

Students, parents and educators have access to all this, and more. The important question is: How do we make the best use of this access in our homes and classrooms? How do we redefine lessons to take advantage of up-to-the minute resources on virtually any topic?

Clearly we can't do this using the model of school we remember from our youth. That model was based on the idea that teachers had the knowledge, and their primary task was to transfer that knowledge to the students.

As I mentioned earlier in this book, the teacher's grip on knowledge was maintained through a variety of devices from burning the printers during the Middle Ages to the "teacher's edition" of textbooks today.

Today that franchise is lost: Any Web site a teacher can visit (at least those I've mentioned) can also be visited by students. The sheer volume of educational information available on the Web eclipses that found in all textbooks combined. Any educator who thinks that this isn't going to change the entire concept of school is sorely mistaken.

But if the role of the teacher is no longer going to be the provider of information, then what will that role be?

We'll explore this topic in a later chapter, but for now it is pretty clear that educators can use the Web to put students to work! Take a look at the CalWeb project (http://www.gsn.org) mentioned above for one way this can happen.

If we want to explore ways for students to become actively engaged learners — to become constructors of their own knowledge — then we need to help them learn how to become Web authors. The next two chapters explore this topic in some depth.

Staking Your Claim on the Web

If you've been exploring the Web, you've probably thought about having a Web presence of your own. Most likely, your ISP will provide you with the space to mount a few of your own Web pages as part of your monthly fee.

How are Web pages created?

The genius of the Web is that all the rich multimedia documents you've seen on the Web are based on plain text files written in HTML: Hypertext Markup Language.

This language uses plain text commands to describe the appearance of a Web page, as well as to contain all the text that appears on the page. Because these documents use standard text files, they can be interpreted on virtually any computer.

What does an HTML file look like?

HTML commands are called "tags." They are enclosed in triangular brackets (<>) and generally appear in pairs. Because an HTML document is plain text, pictures and other media elements are included by reference to their location on the Net relative to the location of the document that uses them. Special characters (such as the cedilla in the Portuguese word, *abraços*) are indicated with special commands so the character appears properly on all computer platforms. Special tags allow any object or text passage to be turned into a link or button that the user clicks on to leap to another Web page, or to another place in the existing document.

155

For example, here is a simple HTML document showing what some of these tags look like, followed by the page's appearance when viewed with Netscape Navigator:

```
<HTML><HEAD>
<TITLE>Sample Page</TITLE>

</HEAD>
<BODY>

<H1>This is a title line</H1>
<P>
<H2>Here is a smaller one</H2>

<CENTER>
<FONT COLOR="0000DD">And now for something fancy, colored
centered text and a table!</FONT>

<TABLE BORDER=2 CELLSPACING=2 CELLPADDING=1><CAPTION
ALIGN=Bottom>English/Portuguese glossary</CAPTION>

<TR>
      <TD>Good morning
      <TD>Bom dia
<TR>
      <TD>Thank you (male)
      <TD>Obrigado
<TR>
      <TD>Tomorrow
      <TD>Amanha
<TR>
      <TD>Hugs
      <TD>AbraÁos
</TABLE>
</CENTER>
To hear these words, you'll first need to have the RealAudio
player.<P>
<P>
<A HREF="http://www.realaudio.com"><IMG SRC="realaudio.gif"
WIDTH=46 HEIGHT=25 ALT="RealAudio icon">Get RealAudio
Now!</A>
</BODY>
</HTML>
```

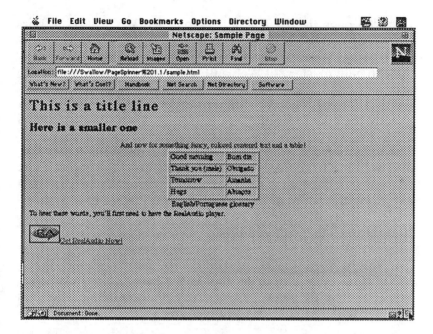

Well, isn't THAT special...

If the correlation between the HTML document and the resulting Web page isn't screamingly obvious to you, don't despair. There are tools (that we will describe soon) to make the task of page creation quite simple.

On the other hand, if you think you can master a handful of commands, you can create the Web pages of your dreams using nothing but a text editor capable of saving files in plain-text format. Since the Web was originally designed by and for the "rocket science" community, the arcane nature of HTML commands was not an issue until fairly recently.

HTML authoring tools

The following authoring tools run the gamut from those that help you work directly with the HTML text files to those that hide all the details and let you work directly with the image of the Web page itself. The latter are called WYSIWYG editors (for What You See Is What You Get).

As you gain mastery of Web authoring (which falls outside the scope of this book) you'll probably adopt a hybrid approach, using different tools for different tasks until your pages look exactly the way to want.

The following list is far from complete. Numerous tools exist, and each has its fervent followers. I've chosen to list just a few to give you the sense of what is out there. Once you start exploring the realm of page creation, you'll want to compare a wider variety of commercial and shareware authoring tools to find the ones that suit you best.

You might think (based on the HTML sample above) that a WYSIWYG page authoring tool is the best choice. After all, you'll be creating pages by working with their appearance, not with the underlying HTML commands.

In fact, this is a powerful approach, and one that might meet all your authoring needs. At the same time, however, there are some tasks for which a smattering of HTML is worth knowing. Fine tuning the look and feel of your pages can make a big difference in how they are perceived, and this fine tuning is still best done with an HTML editor.

We've listed examples of both kinds of Web page tools below — HTML editors and WYSIWYG page creators.

PageSpinner

This excellent program is worth much more than its modest $25 shareware fee. The most recent copy can be found at http://www.shareware.com.

The purpose of this product is to make it easy for you to create Web pages using HTML. You can import an existing text file, for example, and add the HTML marks for headlines, hypertext links, etc. Tables (introduced in Netscape Navigator version 2) can be created simply by selecting the data to be included and clicking on the Table button.

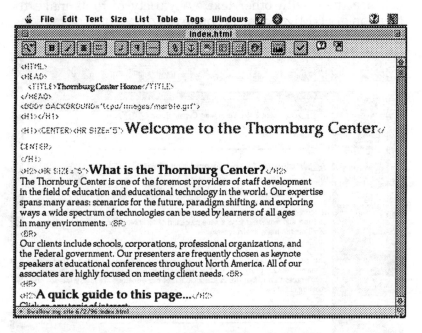

One nice feature of this product is that it lets you know when you are using a feature of HTML that is not standard across all browsers. It also supports JavaScript — small applications embedded in your HTML file that run when the page is loaded.

Another feature worth mentioning is the extensive on-line help provided with this program. If you have even the tiniest smattering of familiarity with HTML, PageSpinner's help tools will have you making professional-caliber pages in no time.

HoT MetaL

Softquad has made version 2.0 of their commercial HTML editing software available for free through their Web site at http://www.sq.com. They believe that, once you get hooked on their product, you'll want to buy the upgrade to version 3.

As with PageSpinner, HoTMetaL is an HTML editor. HTML tags are shown as special graphic elements so you can't confuse them with other text. A variety of tools make the creation of HTML documents quite easy.

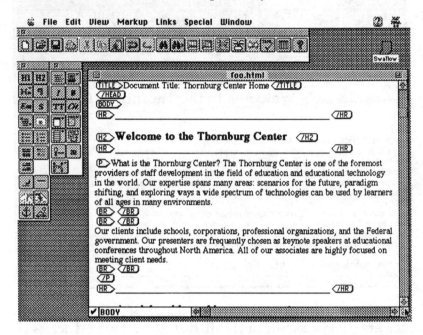

Softquad was one of the pioneers in the creation of HTML editors, and HoTMetaL is a robust tool that has withstood the test of time.

PageMill

This commercial product from Adobe was the first WYSIWYG Web page editor to do a decent job. A demo version of PageMill can be downloaded from http://www.adobe.com.

Even though the first release had a few bugs and produced HTML code that was not as clean as I'd like, I still use it for the bulk of my Web-page design and creation. Tasks that are time consuming, like adding pictures to a page, are trivially easy in PageMill. Instead of locating the path name for a picture, you just simply open the folder containing your pictures, drag the one you want onto the PageMill window and let go! The picture's reference is automatically written to the HTML file as the image appears on the screen.

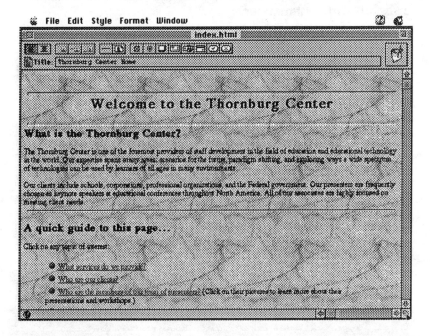

Pages in PageMill look a little different from their appearance in Netscape Navigator or Internet Explorer, but close enough to give a very good idea of what the final result will look like when you use one of these browsers.

The first version lacked support for popular Netscape features like tables, but this is addressed in version 2.0 of this pioneering product.

PageMill will go through frequent upgrades as new capabilities are added to HTML.

Claris Home Page

If you're looking for WYSIWYG HTML editors, Claris Home Page (http://www.claris.com) is worth a close look. It has many similarities to PageMill, although it performs its tasks in a slightly different manner.

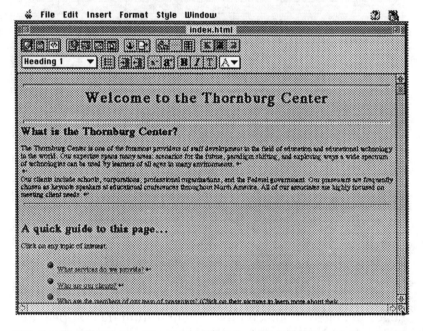

While PageMill has two modes: one for editing and one for previewing a page (very useful for checking local links), Claris Home Page also lets you launch your favorite browser for a complete preview of the page under construction. This is especially valuable when examining special graphics effects such as animations that won't play with the simple preview mode.

One particularly nice feature of this product is its ability to give you an estimated download time for your page, both for 14.4 and 28.8 kb/sec modems.

With the advent of this strong product into the HTML editor race, text-based editors may soon become a fading memory among all but the most persnickity Web page designers.

Netscape Navigator Gold

Netscape has achieved dominance in the Web browser and server markets. They have now decided to add Web authoring tools to their line. The Netscape Gold series of browsers (available at http://www.netscape.com) provide a full-featured browser with the addition of an "Edit" button. The latest "beta" version can be downloaded from their Web site for free.

Once a page is opened in the browser, it can be edited and saved. The user is freed from having to deal with HTML directly. The document looks almost the same in the editor as it does in the browser! One notable exception has to do with image placement. Netscape Navigator supports text-wrap around images. Netscape's editor places the image correctly, but makes you switch from the "edit" to the "browse" mode to see the text wrapping.

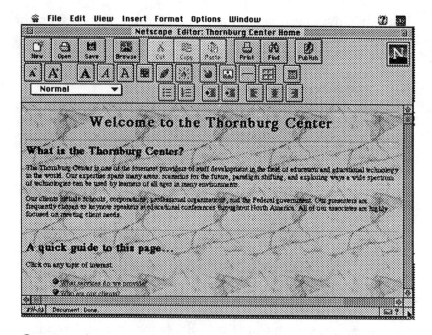

Once you've created your new page, Netscape Gold lets you publish it directly to your Web site without requiring that you use another program to upload the file!

This product is fairly large (the Mac version tips the scales at about 3.5 MB), but it includes a lot of features and offers powerful help tools to show you how to use the various capabilities of the editor.

As of this writing, Netscape Navigator Gold 3.0 is the Swiss Army Knife of Web browsers/editors. As in the past, Netscape keeps raising its own bar!

Web art

The Web started out as a hypertext tool, with an emphasis on the text. With the creation of Mosaic, it rapidly expanded to include graphics. It seems amazing, given the moderately slow connection speeds most people use to navigate the Web, that the rich use of images on Web sites erupted virtually overnight.

While it is true that images can take awhile to load, most of us are patient because we know that images contain information that would be difficult, if not impossible, to convey entirely in words.

Two developments are making images less painful to download. First, high-speed modems are dropping in price, reducing the time needed to download pictures. Second, high-quality image compression techniques make it possible for complex drawings and photographs to make it through phone lines fairly rapidly.

It is commonplace today to use colored background images (automatically supported by most browsers) along with a wide variety of other visual elements that dress up a page to improve its capacity to communicate your message.

Today, most Web browsers support at least two image formats: GIF's and JPEG's. The GIF (Graphical Interchange Format) was originally developed for the Compuserve on-line service. Images saved in this format are highly compressed, but their palette is restricted to a maximum of 256 colors, making this format best suited for line art.

If you want to display photographic images, the JPEG (Joint Photography Expert's Group) format is preferable. Raw images that occupy a megabyte of space can be compressed to well under 100 kB with virtually no visible degradation. The palette can include millions of colors, making these images quite attractive on computers supporting this capability.

Almost all graphics editing programs (such as Adobe Photoshop (http://www.adobe.com)) allow you to save images in either of these compressed formats for inclusion in your Web pages. When your browser encounters one of these image types, it can tell immediately which it is and will display it automatically.

A variation on the standard GIF format (called gif'89) provides two more features that are quite useful for Web authors. The first of these allows you to select one of the 256 colors and make it "transparent." This means that an image with a transparent background would appear on your page without the rectangular frame associated with most images. Web authoring tools like PageMill let you select the color you wish to make transparent for any GIF file you have on your pages.

The second (and more exciting) capacity of the gif'89 format is that it allows the creation of "flip book" animations.

GifBuilder (http://www.shareware.com) allows the creation of animated gif'89 files from a series of still images. All you need to do is create a series of stills using the graphics program of your choice. They should be given names that contain a sequential numbering system (*e.g.*, pict1, pict2, etc.) These pictures are then added to GifBuilder in sequence for assembly into a short movie that plays once, or repeats in a loop.

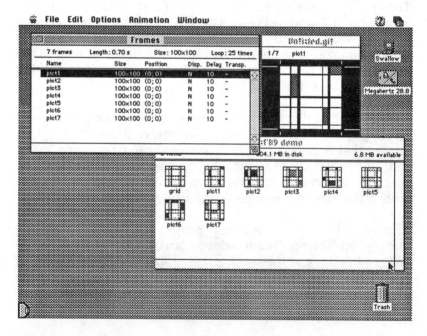

You have lots of choices on frame display time, image placement within the frame, etc., making this quite a versatile tool.

The best part is that your browser most likely already handles animated GIF files, and will play them automatically. If your browser does not know how to play these files, it just displays the first image in the sequence.

You might want to use this feature sparingly. Animation can be overdone, and it should never be used if it clutters up the page.

In addition to GifBuilder, the Web Animator and CelAnimator products mentioned before help bring movement to your pages, so you might want to check them out as well.

Mounting pages

Once you've created your Web masterpiece, you'll have to put it on the Internet in order for anyone to see it!

The first step in this process is to find the location where your pages will be stored. Basically, you'll be sending your files (HTML documents and supporting graphics, sounds, etc.) over the Net to some large hard disk on your server's computer. Many ISP's provide a few megabytes of storage space as part of your monthly fee. While the exact procedure will be shared by your ISP, you'll be provided with three things: The name of a directory where your files will be stored, a "user name" for you to use when logging on to this site, and a password giving you access to the site for storing files.

The second step is to place all of your files in a directory or folder on your computer and to make sure all the images load and that all the local links work by opening your page right from your hard disk using your browser. HTML references are almost always made relative to the page you are opening. If there are problems, this is the best time to fix them. While you are at it, you might want to name your main page "index.html" so this file will be opened by default when someone goes to your directory. In other words, if you visit the Thornburg Center's site at http://www.tcpd.org, you will really be going to a file named "index.html" at this address. Another useful tidbit is to restrict all file names to lowercase only and to make sure there are no spaces in any of the names.

Now you are ready to actually post your pages to the server! This is done using "ftp" — the file transfer protocol. This task can be done within tools like Netscape Navigator Gold, or Apple's Cyberdog. It is more generally performed using dedicated ftp software such as Fetch 3.0 (http://www. shareware.com) for the Macintosh.

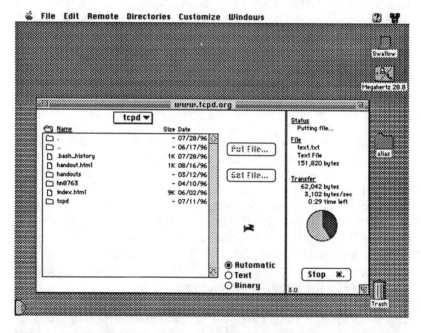

When you load files to your server, you will generally want to have the HTML pages upload as text files, and everything else transfer as "raw binary" files.

Once you're done, go visit your site and see how your page looks. It might take one or two tries to get everything working properly, but you'll soon get used to the process!

Creating a Cybercasting Site

This chapter takes you through the steps needed to turn your Web site into a cybercasting station.

What's in it for you?

Educators who see value in the cybercasting concept can use it at their own sites for student productions. Oral histories can be captured from the grandparents of our students, and these can be used to form an on-line library of stories of our past. During the production of these programs, students acquire interviewing skills, and learn the intricacies of production.

In short, cybercasting is one of the most powerful extensions to your Web site you can provide. It is also one of the easiest to master.

Unlike television, the technology needed to do create audio cybercasts is fairly inexpensive. The only limitation is space on your server and the extent of your imagination.

Technical details

The first few steps in creating audio programs for Web-based delivery are the same as those used for radio production. A program format needs to be chosen (interview, narrative, etc.) and a script or set of questions for a interview must be blocked out. Given my love of "live" broadcasts, I tend to work from an outline rather than from a script, but that just reflects my sweaty-palms approach to life.

How long should the program be?

The answer to this depends on the nature of your topic. Given the realities of transferring files over the Web using cheap modems, I keep my shows to about 15 minutes. This is long enough to explore some interesting ideas, yet short enough to hold people's attention.

Making the recording

The recording should be made with a good tape recorder using decent microphones. The reason for this is that each stage on the production process for cybercasting degrades the original content. Start with the best recording you can make. You don't have to be ridiculous, however. I use a Sony Walkman Pro recorder (http://www.sony.com) with a pair of condenser lapel microphones that cost about $30 apiece. For interviews, my mike is recorded on one stereo channel, and the guest's is recorded in the other. Radio Shack sells an adapter that brings each mike input into a standard stereo phone plug so the whole recording system is quite compact.

I record on high quality tape using Dolby B noise reduction, and make sure the recording level is set properly — neither too low, nor too high. Too high a setting produces distortion that can't be removed later.

The recording location needs to be chosen carefully. For interviews, I'm usually at airports, hotels, or conference centers — not in recording studios. While a certain amount of background noise lends a sense of presence to the recording, be careful to record in as quiet a setting as possible. Bowling alleys, for example, are off my list as recording sites, as are video game parlors.

Once the show is on tape, the rest of the production is pretty easy. Basically, you have to transfer the audio file from your tape recorder to your computer. In addition to your tape recorder, you'll want another piece of equipment: an audio mixer. The purpose of this device is to take each of the channels of your recording (two, for my interviews, for example) and mix them down into a single audio channel for transfer to the computer. During this process, you can adjust the volume levels for each channel, and change the equalization (high-tech jargon for treble and bass settings) for optimal playback from your Web page.

My favorite mixer is the Mackie 1202 — a professional mixer that is very affordable for schools and home-based studios. As with your recorder, you'll want the best mixer you can afford just to keep from adding any noise or distortion to the signal.

Getting the audio into your computer

Once you have your tape recorder hooked to your mixer, and the mixer hooked to your computer, you are ready to turn your audio tape into a digital recording.

There are lots of audio recording programs on the market ranging in price from free to prohibitively expensive. If you are keeping with the spirit of live radio (especially AM-quality audio with little or no music), the free option works just great.

What you want is a recording program that records directly to your hard disk instead of your computer's RAM. The reason for this is that you'll want your digital master to be recorded at 16-bits of resolution at 22 kHz — a moderately high-quality setting that eats up a few megabytes per minute. Unless you have an unlimited RAM budget, you'll want to just spool this audio right to your hard drive. The Iomega ZIP drive (http://www.iomega.com) is perfect for this task, and the 100 megabyte cartridges are only about $15 each.

I do my recording on a Macintosh using SoundMachine 2.2.2 (http://online.anu.edu.au/RSISE/teleng/Software/welcome. html) and save the audio as an "AIFF" file. This platform-independent standard is best suited for direct recording to disk. While SoundMachine 2.2.2 is an old shareware program, lacking many of the features I treasure in audio recording software, it is reliable and records directly to the hard drive.

I expect other quality audio recording programs that spool to disk will become available as shareware soon.

As with the original recording, set the level carefully. Too high a recording level produces distortion. Your mixer will let you balance the volume of the host and the guest (for an interview) so they both record at the same volume level. Experiment with level settings by recording a few minutes from the tape, then play it back. If the audio sounds scratchy or clipped, you probably have the recording level set too high. Be careful at the other end as well. Recording at too low a level makes the sounds hard to hear. A bit of experimentation will provide just the right balance.

Preparing the file for the Web

Given the fact that most of our clients access the Web with phone-based connections using a 14.4 or 28.8 kb/sec modem, it would be foolish to place a 30-50 megabyte file on my site, no matter how compelling the content.

Fortunately, this is not an issue. Companies like RealAudio (http://www.realaudio.com) have developed special compression and playback tools geared to the realities of today's Web.

As a supplier of cybercast material, you'll need two pieces of software — both available for free from RealAudio. The first of these is the RealAudio conversion program that translates your huge AIFF file to a very compact, but high quality, file based on the RealAudio (.ra) sound format. This program is fairly easy to use. It allows you to enter information about the recording that appears on the user's screen during playback, and it gives you two choices for audio quality. The highest quality setting is for playback on 28.8 kb/sec modems or faster. I use the lower setting for 14.4 kb/sec modems instead. This results in more compact files (reducing download time) yet still produces adequate quality audio for voice. The resulting sound quality is similar to an AM radio playing through a small speaker.

You'll also need a copy of the RealAudio player software, as will your listeners. You can provide a link to RealAudio's site so your users can get the player software if they don't already have it.

If you set your site up so people will download the audio file before playing it, this is all you'll need. Before posting any files to your site, however, be sure to contact your service provider to be sure they have set up the RealAudio "MIME type" on their server. This is a simple, but essential, way to insure that when a user clicks on one of your files it downloads properly.

RealAudio's instructions are quite clear, and it took only two tries before I had everything working smoothly!

Streaming vs. downloading

An alternative playback method supported by RealAudio is called "streaming." Instead of downloading the file before playing it, a "streaming playback" plays sounds as the file is being read. This is essential for live broadcasts, and has its place for archived materials as well. In order to support this feature, your service provider will need to install the RealAudio server software on their host computer.

Since many of our users pay for their own access, we opted for the "download" method because a 15-minute program can be downloaded using a 28.8 kb/sec modem in about 5 minutes.

Once downloaded, the file can be played back off-line, and even copied to a floppy to be given to someone else.

As with much of the recent evolution of the Web, cybercasting opens new creative doors for all of us. It has long been said that the power of the press belongs to those who own them. With a bit of free software and some creativity, you can own your own cybercasting station!

A Digression on Car Buying

Sun Microsystems provides workshops on the impact of the Web in business throughout the country. At each of these the following mantra is repeated: If your business isn't on the Web today, you'll be out of business tomorrow.

Is this just self-serving propaganda? Should business be on the Web in order to survive? What can the Web offer customers, employees, suppliers, dealers? More to the point, is anyone making any money yet?

Let me answer by way of a personal story:

In the Spring of 1996 I was driving home to the San Francisco area from Sacramento, CA in my Mazda RX-7 when it overheated and blew out the engine. (Aluminum engines have no tolerance for overheating, I found.)

I was getting ready for a new car anyway, since mine had 200,000 miles on it; but I dreaded the car buying process — especially haggling for the best price.

My initial plan was to get a new RX-7, but they aren't made any more. I was really stuck! I hadn't looked at cars in years, and had no idea what I should be buying.

A friend loaned me an old car while I was looking so I wouldn't just buy the first car I saw. As I drove around, I noticed several cars that looked promising and made a list.

My next step was to go on the Net and search for information on each of the cars I'd seen. The most useful resource I came across was the Edmunds site (http://www.edmunds.com).

This site had detailed information on new and used cars, and seemed to list just about very car on the road today.

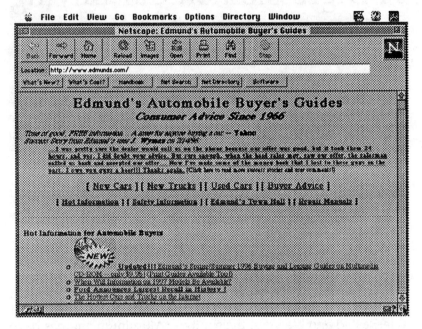

One of its truly great features was a list of the "invoice" and actual dealer cost for each car, broken down for each option. By looking up information on used cars in each model, I found a historical base of customer satisfaction information that was quite useful.

I printed out all the information on each car and then visited a few dealers to see what these cars looked like. As soon as the salesmen saw me come in with my own printouts, all the high-pressure façade fell away: They knew I was doing my homework and wouldn't stick around to hear their "great deal" when I knew what the car actually cost them.

It was during one of these visits that I tried a car I really liked. After the test drive, the dealer asked if I'd be back. I told him that I would be if his dealership was listed in the Web-based buying service I was using. (It wasn't, so he lost the sale.)

My next step was to go back to the Edmunds site and click on the Auto-by-Tel (http://www.autobytel.com) button. I filled out a detailed form telling exactly what car I wanted, down to the last option. Within two days I received an e-mail message listing a dealer in my area who would give me a firm price over the phone. Furthermore, I was told that if the price or service from this dealer wasn't to my liking, I should contact Auto by Tel!

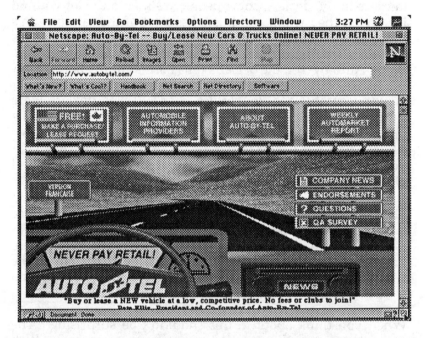

The dealer knew that I had a copy of their actual vehicle cost in my hands. I called the dealer, he quoted $200 over their cost (almost $3,000 under sticker price), and we had a deal. This "negotiation" took all of five minutes, most of which was spent telling me how to get to his lot.

After buying the car, I asked the dealer how he liked selling cars this way. He showed me a binder almost one-inch thick with sales they had made this way in the first four months of the year.

The Web turned my car buying experience into a win-win situation. In fact, the experience is so good that some car dealers in Texas succeeded in outlawing the Auto-by-Tel service for awhile because they felt it cutting into their traditional high-pressure (high-markup) sales.

As you might have guessed, the markup on cars can be quite high — up to fifteen thousand dollars in some cases. In fairness to the dealers, some people walk onto the lot with no idea what they want, and this takes a lot of the salesperson's time. The National Automobile Dealer's Association figures that it takes about $307 of a dealer's time to close a sale. Using Auto-by-Tel, the dealer's time cost is cut to about $25.

How successful has the service been? Texas dealers were selling between 3,000 and 6,000 cars a month through the program when the state shut it down there. Surely Texas' citizens will put a stop to the lunacy of having the state shut down a Web-based buying service that meets their needs and gives them a great price.

The important message is that substantial Net-based commerce is not over some distant horizon — it is here today. Forrester Research figures that $300 million in goods and services were purchased over the Net last year. This number is a tad on the short side: Auto-by-Tel's sales have been running $280 million — each month!

When you think about it, this shouldn't be surprising. The current demographics of Web-users favor commerce: Web users have higher than average income and are sophisticated enough to research major purchases on their own.

If the Auto-by-Tel trend continues, successful dealerships may someday consist of a small fleet of demo cars and a service department. A handful of order takers could process all the sales, and the car could be delivered directly from the factory to the customer's door.

No wonder the traditional car dealerships feel threatened!

What does this have to do with education? The next chapter explores that topic!

Disintermediation

The twin revolutions of silicon and glass are turning much of our world upside down. Improved silicon-based integrated circuits enable today's personal computers to perform better than the monstrous mainframes of only a few years ago. Fiber-optic systems — capable of sending the peak load of phone calls on Mother's Day down a strand of glass the diameter of a human hair — are revolutionizing broadband communications. By linking these powerful computers and communication tools, the information-rich world of the Web becomes ubiquitously accessible.

One can hardly watch an advertisement on television today without seeing an invitation to visit the sponsor's Web-site. Ad's blare out the "URL's" of company after company.

Why the push? Why are advertisers playing to a minority audience of (generally) upscale computer owners? For the same reason Willie Sutton robbed banks: "That's where the money is."

In 1994 Americans spent more money purchasing computers than television sets. In 1995, the actual number of computers sold exceeded the number of new televisions purchased. According to Intel's Andy Grove, this will be true world-wide by 1997. Furthermore, half of our existing home computers (and virtually all of the new ones) have modems in them to provide access to the Net.

And, everyone with a modem has a weapon to wipe out the middle-man. The key word to remember is "disintermediation" — it will influence many aspects of your world very soon.

Look at software distribution for example. In the pre-Net days, a software publisher would produce a title, typeset a manual, design a flashy package, manufacture the product in volume, place it with a distributor (at 60% off list price) who would then get the product to retailers where its sales were largely dependent on customers walking in off the street looking for the title. It is rare to find a software retailer whose sales force knows anything significant about the products on display.

Because of this, many excellent products languish on the shelves until the space is needed for the Next Great Thing, at which point the remaining inventory is returned to the distributor who then ships it back to the manufacturer who then scraps it. Old versions of popular titles get shipped back the minute a new revision becomes available.

With the Web as a marketplace, software companies can deal directly with their customers, completely bypassing the distribution and retail channels.

Forefront Group provides an excellent case history in this regard: A demo version of their stellar product, Webwhacker, can be downloaded from their site (http://www.ffg.com). Potential customers have 30 days to try out the product before deciding whether to purchase it. If the customer finds the product valuable, a quick phone, fax, or Net-based transaction seals the purchase on a charge card. A special password is then sent to the customer's e-mail address and he or she is then allowed to download the complete product with full documentation.

The customer buys the program for a fraction of the retail price this product would command in a retail store. The discount to the distributor and retailer is passed onto the customer.

Note the benefits that come from selling software this way:

- The customer gets to try the product before purchasing it.
- The supplier has no physical inventory to maintain.
- The customer gets a great price.

- The supplier knows the name and (e-mail) address of every customer — useful information when updates and other products come out.

The only losers in this transaction are the retailer and distributor. They have been disintermediated out of this company's sales cycle.

While disintermediation works for software, what about other products?

Take blue jeans, for example. A visitor to Levi's Web site (http://www.levi.com) is provided with the tools needed to order a perfect pair of jeans. Today their site sends you to a store to order your Personal Pair, but in the future, by following the measurement instructions and placing a order directly with the company, these custom jeans could be crafted and shipped directly to the client. No retailer, no inventory, no scrap, nothing but a pair of properly fitted jeans.

This model of mass customization can be carried further. Chrysler (http://www.chrysler.com) provides an on-line showroom highlighting its latest products. In the future, after looking at the features list, a customer will be able to specify exactly the car he or she wants. This car will be custom-built and delivered to the customer within weeks.

By the end of the century, cars will probably be delivered within three days.

Stock research (http://www.quote.com) and trades (http://www.etrade.com) are available on the Web today.

Airline tickets (http://www.cntraveler. com) and hotel reservations (http://www.all-hotels.com) are available on-line with the savings passed on to the customer.

What is the role of stock brokerage firms, clothing stores, car dealerships, and other retail establishments in a world of net-based transactions?

The new role hinges on the words "value-added." Unless the business offers enough to the customer to justify the profit margin, the customer will bypass the traditional channel in an instant. Some retailers and distributors will rise to the challenge, while others will not. Those who fail to find ways to bring extra value or service to their customers will be out of business.

And this brings me to our main topic, education — specifically to the institution we call school.

Textbooks are designed to maintain information control in the hands of the teachers by insuring that the teacher's copy of the textbook has more information than the child's copy. This, coupled with a lockstep curriculum, creates an environment where student inquiry is discouraged and is occasionally treated as aberrant behavior.

One consequence of this model is that many students dislike school, even if they still love learning. Accordingly, schools (along with prisons and mental hospitals) are the only places where, if you don't go, they came and get you.

Even today, most teachers bemoan the fact that children spend more hours watching television than they spend in classrooms.

From the standpoint of "information delivery," educators are tremendously outpaced by the combined horsepower of television and the Web.

Without trying to compete with schools, Discovery Channel (http://www.discovery.com) probably provides more in-depth coverage of the life sciences than many K-12 schools. The History Channel does the same for social studies — and other cable channels contribute as well. All these channels owe a debt to PBS for its pioneering role in using television to inform and educate, as well as entertain.

186

Add this rich panoply of programming to the power of the Web, and the impact is staggering.

As we've shown in a previous chapter, the American Memory Project at the Library of Congress (http://www.loc.gov) contains many thousands of photographs and other documents relating to our country's history — all free for the taking. The Web Museum in Paris (http://www.emf.net/louvre) contains a rich collection of fine art from hundreds of artists dating from pre-renaissance to post-modern periods. High-resolution color images and essays on the artists and their works can be downloaded by learners for free.

In addition to raw material, students can take courses — for free — from a variety of institutions ranging from high schools to community colleges and corporate training centers. Sun Microsystems, for example, is moving its entire staff development program on-line, and is making many of its offerings available to the public at no cost (http://www.sun.com/sunergy).

Recall that the Web is doubling every 90 days, and you can only imagine what educational content will be on-line next month, let alone next year.

Before we toss schools onto the scrap heap of history as yet another casualty in the disintermediation onslaught, we need to revisit the only safeguard available: value-added. If schools are unable to demonstrate enough added-value, they risk becoming irrelevant to the educational enterprise, and will cease to exist.

Fortunately (for schools) added-value can be found. I found it in a wonderful poem on the loss of spirituality by T. S. Eliot — a poem called The Rock.

In the first stanza Eliot asks:

Where is the life we've lost in living?
Where is the wisdom we've lost in knowledge?
Where is the knowledge we've lost in information?

These lines hold (I think) the key to redefining schools in ways that will make them desirable places for learners to congregate — even if they aren't forced to attend.

For all its richness, PBS (http://www.pbs.org), Discovery Channel (http://www.discovery.com), CNN (http://cnn.com) and the other excellent programming options available in the bulk of our homes, offer only information. The billions of words and images and sounds and movies on the Web offer only information.

The task of educators (and schools) becomes that of running Eliot's words backward. It is human beings in the form of passionate teachers who help students find the knowledge we've lost in information; who help us find the wisdom we've lost in knowledge; and who, most importantly of all, who help us find the life we've lost in living.

Schools that rise to this challenge will flourish. Those that don't deserve to shut down. As I've said on numerous occasions, any teacher who can be replaced by a computer should be.

Like television before it, the Net isn't going away. It is up to educational institutions at all levels to redefine their role in an Web-wise world.

Education in a Post-Gutenberg World

Before ending this book, I want to spend a little time exploring the future. Everything I've written about so far has either already happened, or will happen in very short order. The advance of technology is rapid and ruthless.

But institutions do not change as quickly as technologies. Educators have a special challenge in dealing with change. For one thing, their students are products of the new generation — generation.com — a cadre of Web-ready learners for whom the linear confines of outdated textbooks are as anachronistic as quill pens. It is this generation who stands ready to take advantage of Vannevar Bush's memex machine, only it won't be in a desk as he envisioned.

The Web-tool for our youth will be a true personal computer. A compact machine that is no longer tied to the desk with the twin cords of electrical power and a phone line — a compact wireless device that brings true "anywhere, anytime" Web access to all learners wherever they may be, whenever they want to use it.

Back in the 1970's, one of my colleagues at the Xerox Palo Alto Research Center, Alan Kay, promoted the idea of a "Dynabook" — a truly portable computer that learners could carry with them for use anytime they wished. Like Bush's memex, this machine would contain vast libraries that students could search and from which they could make connections as they created documents of their own.

Today's memex does not need to have vast libraries on-board — they are a mouse-click away in cyberspace. These libraries are doubling in size every three months, and we are in the midst of an information explosion unknown in history.

The challenge, as I see it, is not the creation of the compact computers that students will use to navigate through this digital domain — the Apple Newton and its offspring point a way toward that goal, especially as DEC (the microprocessor vendor for the Newton) has just released a new cheap processor that has a throughput of over one billion operations per second. No, the challenge comes from another source — tools for navigating through informational spaces.

In an earlier chapter we explored a variety of search tools for the Internet — tools that locate relevant documents or sites based on your interests. These tools are still in their early stages of development, and they are improving every month. No matter how powerful they become, these search tools will fail to meet some of our needs for one simple reason: In order to use them you need to know what you don't know.

In other words, you need to know enough about the topic you are exploring to ask the right questions. In a traditional school setting this isn't a problem. Teachers will probably make the move from telling the students the information they need to know to telling them the questions they need to ask in order to find this information themselves.

While this is a step in the right direction, it doesn't go far enough. Informational repositories as large as the Web are too vast to explore using just logical searches. To get an idea of why this is the case, let me tell you how I use my local library. I usually go to the library with a specific task in mind. A few minutes on the library computer is all it takes for me to find the books I went there to check out.

Something happens as I walk through the stacks. Sometimes I end up on the wrong floor, and spend a few minutes browsing the collections in front of me — often to great benefit. Even when I get to the "right" area, I take my books and then browse the adjacent shelves to see what looks interesting.

The only reason I can do this is because my local library is quite small — probably under 100,000 volumes.

But how does one find serendipity in a library with millions of volumes scattered all over the world? Instead of using the "sneakernet" in our trips down aisles of books, we need a spaceship for cyberspace navigation. This ship would allow us to zoom through informational spaces, presenting us with incredible amounts of information that just catches our consciousness. Such tools provide a gestalt of cyberspace — a perceived wholeness of a world that is, in reality, nothing more that bits of information scattered on hard drives in garages, universities, schools, libraries, businesses and homes. Like Alice venturing through the looking glass, we cyberspace adventurers could pass through our computer monitors to the other side ... to touch the information itself.

Several projects are currently exploring new ways of navigating through informational spaces. One of the more promising is a research program at Apple called Project X (http://mcf.research.apple.com/ProjectX).

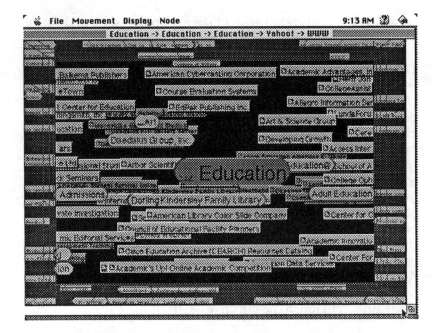

Education → Education → Education → Yahoo! → WWW

This tool allows you to sail through a three-dimensional representation of cyberspace, where depth represents the various sub-levels at which information is stored. By using the mouse and keyboard as your navigational tool, you can get a global overview of a particular informational space (the Yahoo directory, for example) and then zoom in on those items you want to explore in detail. Once you've found a destination of interest, a single mouse click launches your browser and takes you to that site.

Project X shows that the development of models for getting information about information can be as exciting as getting the information itself.

But what about our young people? How will they react to an educational environment in which anything they could want to know about is available to them in formats that honor their individual learning styles?

Some will react quite well, and others will not. Many students today are so used to teachers telling them what they need to know that they will become disequilibrated in this brave new world. They will need guides to take them across the bridges of discovery — they need their teachers, their parents, their community leaders, their business leaders, and their peers. They need a culture that values learning. And most of all, the need a climate that cares.

The Web is a powerful tool for education, but that is all it is. It is the physical web of people in the lives of our learners that makes the real difference.

Glossary of Terms

Every craft has its jargon, and the world of computers and communication is no exception. The following brief glossary defines a few of the terms you are likely to encounter in this book and during your ongoing adventures into cyberspace.

aiff: A sound file format.

au: A UNIX sound file format.

Anchor: A synonym for hyperlink.

Bandwidth: The capacity of a communication line to carry information (measured in bits/sec).

Baud: The speed at which modems transfer data. One baud is roughly equal to one bit per second. It takes eight bits to make up one letter or character. Modems rarely transfer data at exactly the same speed as their listed baud rate because of static or computer problems.

Browser: A World Wide Web client. An information retrieval tool. Netscape Navigator is an example of a browser.

CERN: The European Laboratory for Particle Physics. The originators of the HTTP and HTML concepts.

Client: The software that allows users the ability to retrieve information from the Internet and World Wide Web.

Cyberspace: A word coined by William Gibson in his sci-fi classic, *Neuromancer*, to describe the Net. Today the word is commonly used to describe the universe of electronic information represented by all the interconnected networks, and computers scattered all over the world. Once you start exploring the Net yourself, you will probably notice that it has a feeling of "placeness" to it.

Download: Copy a file from a host system to your computer. There are several different methods, or protocols, for downloading files, most of which periodically check the file as it is being copied to ensure no information is inadvertently destroyed or damaged during the process. Some, such as XMODEM, only let you download one file at a time. Others, such as batch-YMODEM and ZMODEM, let you type in the names of several files at once, which are then automatically downloaded.

E-mail: Electronic mail — a way to send a private message to somebody else on the Net. Used as both noun and verb.

FAQ: Frequently Asked Questions. A compilation of answers to these. Many Usenet newsgroups have these files, which are posted once a month or so for beginners.

Freeware: Software that doesn't cost anything.

FTP: File-Transfer Protocol. A system for transferring files across the Net. Sometimes this term is used as a verb: "To get this picture, just ftp to photo.si.edu." Anonymous ftp sites are available for public access file retrieval, although sometimes access is restricted to certain times of the day.

GIF: Graphics Interchange Format, an image file format. This format is particularly well suited for non-photographic art — line drawings, etc.

GIF'89: A variant of the GIF format that supports transparency and the ability to play back a collection of frames as a movie.

Gopher: A menu-driven navigational tool for finding resources on the Internet.

Helper Application: a program used by the browser when it cannot handle a particular file type internally. When your browser encounters on of these files it will pass it to a helper application that will display the file to the user.

History List: A list of Document Titles and URLs your browser keeps in memory that represents the visited URLs during a given Web session.

Home Page: A top level HTML document that a user frequently visits. This document is usually displayed when you start a Web session.

Host system: A public-access site providing Net access to people outside the research and government community.

Hotlist: a user defined list of preferred URLs to a given World Wide Web document.

HTML: HyperText Markup Language. The rules that govern the way we create documents so that they can be read by a WWW Browser. Most documents that are displayed by browsers are HTML documents. These are characterized by the .html or .htm file extension. For example: homepage.html or homepage.htm. (Note: .html is commonly used as an extension for Web pages mounted on Macintosh or UNIX-based servers. Those using Microsoft software are restricted to three characters after the "dot" (.), hence ".htm."

HTTP: HyperText Transport Protocol, the protocol used by the WWW servers.

Hyperlink: A link in a given document to information within another document. These links are usually represented by highlighted words or images. The user also has the option to underline these hyperlinks.

Hypermedia: richly formatted documents containing a variety of information types, such as textual, image, movie, and audio. These information types are easily found through hyperlinks.

In-line image: a graphic image that is displayed with an HTML document.

Internet: A worldwide system for linking smaller computer networks together. Networks connected through the Internet use a particular set of communications standards to communicate, known as TCP/IP.

JPEG: Joint Photographic Expert Group, a method of storing an image in digital format. This format is especially good for images based on photographs or video.

Listserv: A tool for distributing messages to a list of subscribers who have a shared interest in some subject. Once a message is sent to the list server, copies are immediately sent to everyone on the list.

Log off: Disconnect from a host system.

Log on/log in: Connect to a host system or public-access site.

Lurk: To browse a subscribed newsgroup without posting anything.

Mailing list: Essentially a conference in which messages are delivered right to your mailbox, instead of to a Usenet newsgroup. You get on these by sending a message to a specific e-mail address, which is often that of a computer that automates the process.

MIME: Multiple Internet Mail Extensions, a method of identifying files such that the first packet of information received by a client, contains information about the type of file the server has sent. For example text, audio, movie, postscript, etc....

NCSA: The National Center for Supercomputing Applications. NCSA is located at the University of Illinois in Urbana-Champaign, Illinois.

Net: Another way of referring to the Internet.

Network: A communications system that links two or more computers. It can be as simple as a cable strung between two computers a few feet apart or as complex as hundreds of thousands of computers around the world linked through fiber optic cables, phone lines and satellites.

Newsgroup: A Usenet conference.

On-line: When your computer is connected to an on-line service, bulletin-board system or public-access site.

Plug-in: An application that extends the capability of your your browser to explore documents of various types.

Post: To compose a message for a Usenet newsgroup and then send it out for others to see.

PostScript: A page description language developed by Adobe Systems.

Protocol: A planned method of exchanging data over the Internet.

QuickTime: A method of storing movie and audio files in a digital format.

Server: A computer that houses Web sites and/or can distribute information or files automatically in response to specifically worded e-mail requests.

SGML: Standard Generalized Markup Language, is an International standard, a encoding scheme for creating textual information. HTML is a subset of SGML.

Shareware: Software that is freely available on the Net, but which, if you like and use it, you should pay for by sending in the fee requested by the author, whose name and address will be found in a file distributed with the software.

Snail mail: Mail that comes through a slot in your front door.

TCP/IP: Transmission Control Protocol/Internet Protocol, a set of rules that establish the method by which data is transmitted over the Internet between two computers.

Telnet: A program that lets you connect to other computers on the Internet.

URL: Uniform Resource Locator, the address to a source of information. The URL contains four distinct parts, the protocol type, the machine name, the directory path and the file name. For example: http://www.tcpd.org/tcpd/perspectives.html

Usenet newsgroup: A repository of "news" items ranging from messages to pictures, sounds, movies, and computer software. Subscribers are notified when new material germane to their interest is posted. They then access the items from the newsgroup itself. Unlike listservs, newsgroups are stored in a central location rather than sent to every subscriber as e-mail.

Veronica: A program that searches Gopher servers based on keywords provided by the user.

World Wide Web: (WWW, W3, The Web): A distributed HyperText-based information system conceived at CERN to provide its user community an easy way to access global information.

References

Marshall McLuhan and Bruce Powers, *The Global Village: Transformations in World Life and Media in the 21st Century,* Oxford, 1989.
Marshall McLuhan, *Gutenberg Galaxy,* Mentor Books, 1962.
Marshall McLuhan, *Understanding Media: The Extensions of Man,* Signet, 1964.
Neil Postman, *Technopoly, The Surrender of Culture to Technology,* Vintage Books, 1993.
Neil Postman, *The End of Education,* Knopf, 1995.
Don Tapscott, *Digital Economy,* McGraw Hill, 1995.
David Thornburg, *Education in the Communication Age,* Starsong, 1994.